Secrets
to Ongoing
Success

Keeping Yourself and Your Organization Fresh

BRUCE REINSTEIN

Praise for Secrets to Ongoing Success

SECRETS TO ON GOING SUCCESS is a masterful blend of experience and wisdom for making money as told by the author who has spent a career, spanning decades, in the foodservice and hospitality business. There's more than a hundred tips throughout the pages of this book. You will get some big brain ideas on how to look at your business through a different lens and continually make business improvements for winning!

— **Kathy Doyle, president and publisher Fastcasual.com QSRweb.com**

The restaurant industry, and business in general continues to evolve but being able to adjustment and do things the right way remains a constant for current and future leaders. The author articulated this point throughout his book by allowing the reader to visualize his experiences so they can use them to become better managers themselves. The message is to use the 34 chapters and think about how you can move forward in your career by being different which he emphasizes while also being ethical. I believe strongly in "teaching and learning "and Bruce does a masterful job teaching what right looks like. An organization would certainly benefit by having him "teach" at their corporate seminars.

— **Frank Guidara, Former CEO Au Bon Pain, Pizzeria UNO and Wolfgang Puck Food Co.**

I have been in hospitality my entire career. But more than a career it has been my life having grown up walking the halls of my Dad's hotel office as a kid. Since Bruce grew up in the business in a very similar fashion, inevitability we share a unique perspective on what it takes to succeed. Learning is a path and never a destination, and Bruce knows this and speaks to this in his terrific new book. I enjoyed reading some of his anecdotal stories which ring so true to me. He speaks about learning (with his team), loving (with his wife) and his relentless energy in creating success in business and in life. This book is enjoyable, educational and inspirational. An easy read that will get the reader focused on what it takes to compete and succeed in one of the most challenging businesses on earth!

— **Jeffrey Saunders, CEO Saunders Hotel Group**

"In the restaurant business today, success comes not so much from capitalizing on what's new, but rather what's next. The author brings the reader along as he retraces his multi-path journey to the top in the restaurant industry. Along the way, he shares solid, proven business insights, talks about missteps, and mixes in just the right amount of professional learnings, soulful anecdotes, and personal insights that will show you the tried-and-true path to ongoing success."

— **Gerald White, Associate Publisher Plate Magazine**

I very much enjoyed Bruce Reinstein's book. As a Founder and CEO of a growing restaurant brand. Bruce's book replicates the process that I have gone through for over 45 years in the business, and over 22 years building our business from scratch. Let him highlight for you the opportunities and challenges as you grow your business. His dedication and passion for our business shows through the many stories of his long career. Hopefully you can use his template to shortcut the many pitfalls that exist in operating a restaurant and enjoy a long and lasting successful entry into our industry.

— **Bruce Dean, Co-founder/CEO Black Bear Diner**

Publisher's Cataloging-in-Publication data

Reinstein, Bruce.
Secrets to Ongoing Success: Keeping yourself and your organization fresh /Bruce Reinstein.

Edited by Valerie Killifer

Print ISBN: 978-1-54392-931-7

eBook ISBN: 978-1-54392-932-4

1. The main category of the book —Self Improvement —Other category. 2. Another subject category —Business. 3. More categories —Hospitality

HF0000.A0 A00 2010
299.000 00–dc22 2010999999
First Edition
14 13 12 11 10 / 10 9 8 7 6 5 4 3 2 1

TABLE OF CONTENTS

INTRODUCTION

Success is never a given and when you achieve success, it is measured very differently by most people. For some, success is strictly financial, while for others, it is about fame and recognition. But, what does success mean for you? The answer may be quite varied at different times, but one thing is for sure: Everyone is at a different stage in their lives and there will be many professional and personal wins along each person's individual path. There also will be many more obstacles. How you deal with those obstacles will define who you will become and whether your success will be ongoing.

Keeping yourself fresh involves surrounding yourself with great people, who in many cases provide you with strengths that you do not have. The underlying question that has helped shape the great teams that I have been a part of will always be "What do you think?" It forces people to evaluate themselves as well as the person who asked the question. They will then begin the process of defining who they are and who you are to them. Leadership involves challenging yourself and others. By asking your team what they think, you are getting them involved in decisions. Even if you believe they are off base, you can use their responses as a teaching moment. At the same time, great ideas from others can transform you and keep you thinking ahead.

This book will take you through the story of how you got to where you are today and where you have taken some miss-steps. Most important, is how you will adapt at the end of the book. You will define (or re-define) your future after reading each chapter and reviewing the key takeaways. It does not matter how old you are or what you have accomplished so far. It is about how you define who you are moving forward. It is time to re-energize yourself, the people around you and your business. It is time to be different, so that you avoid being measured by being better. And, it is time to continue to develop yourself and your team by challenging the status quo.

Watch everything around you, ask lots of questions and be a great listener. If you do this, I promise that you will keep yourself and your organization ahead of the curve.

Happy Reading,

We live in a world of constant pressure to be better than someone else. Competition in school, sports, work and socially creates levels of pressure that do not need to always exist. Being different is what sets you apart. If you focus on being different, your world will change dramatically for the better.

PART ONE

WHO AM I?

1

A LOOK IN THE MIRROR

Being different all starts with how you look at yourself. It's what makes you unique and is what separates you from the rest of the world. However, to be different, we must be willing to learn, to grow and to try new things.

Throughout the next 34 chapters, I am going to tell you stories based on my experiences and the experiences of others in the industry. Keep in mind there are different endings to each story with a clear message to be learned from each outcome.

Realistically, both success and failure come with their own set of pitfalls and each do not last long for most. But how you deal with success and failure falls on you, and is where you can begin to differentiate yourself from everyone else. Keep in mind that differentiation is not about being better than everyone else. That is a mindset that will get you into trouble more times than not. Rather, the willingness to always improve on what you already have is where true long-term success begins.

Getting better at everything is not the same as being better. You want to constantly get better to differentiate yourself and your brand. Yes, being different will make you successful long term, but the idea of being better fosters a sense of superiority that will lead to short-term gain and long-term failure.

Keep in mind that stagnation is the biggest enemy to long term success. It is caused by massive egos and the feeling that you are superior to others in every way. However, when you start asking the right questions, truly listening to the answers and taking the correct course of action, you can get better each day.

We go to school for many years to learn, but our academic education is a small part of what we learn and who we become. My father used to tell me that he was "street smart." It took me a while to understand what he meant, but I now live every day with an openness to learn. While none of us are perfect at anything, we can be different than the rest.

Keep in mind that this is not a lecture! We are officially becoming a team, throughout this book. My whole career has been based on a team environment. I learned from bosses and fellow employees and then I learned from my employees to become a better boss. It does not matter the level of experience. Every person brings something to the table that will make you better. And I learned this by watching my dad.

From Howdy Beefburger to Souper Salad

Dave was my father. Everyone knew Dave and liked him, and in 1976 he opened a 400-square-foot restaurant in the financial district of Boston called Souper Salad. He was 50 years old and his previous business, Howdy Beefburger, had closed. Dave relied on his friends to help him get this new restaurant opened. As he said later: "I did not have two nickels to open anything." But, the concept was simple: a bottomless salad bar and 10 daily soups with many of the products made on premises.

It was tough going for him early on; however, the key to his success was that he got to know every customer. Eventually, they came in to see him as much as they came in to have their lunch. Many of these customers would follow him as the financial district exploded in Boston and Souper Salad started to open throughout the city. He was planting the seed and not taking this business for granted. This one location would never be enough to make him financially successful, but he was learning and growing as the business expanded. The Souper Salad concept was different at the time, yet it would need to be reinvented many times along the way to maintain brand longevity.

While my father was opening this 400-square-foot restaurant and starting over at 50, he also was putting me through college at Cornell. Dave's dream was to have his three sons in business with him, but my dream at the time was to work in the hotel industry. My dad supported this and while I spent many years working in the industry that gave me a start, my dad's dream would also eventually come true. But that is another story to be told later.

Michael Jackson said it all in his song, "Man in the mirror." Read the words. We can all make a difference; we just need to make changes where warranted. My dad changed his dream to support mine while I learned all I could from the hotel industry in order to support his. And while we can all change some of the words in Michael Jackson's song to fit them into our own lives, the message is clear. Change starts with us.

"I'm Gonna Make A Change,
For Once In My Life
It's Gonna Feel Real Good,
Gonna Make A Difference
Gonna Make It Right . . .

As I, Turn Up The Collar On My
Favourite Winter Coat
This Wind Is Blowin' My Mind
I See The Kids In The Street,
With Not Enough To Eat
Who Am I, To Be Blind?
Pretending Not To See
Their Needs
A Summer's Disregard,
A Broken Bottle Top
And A One Man's Soul
They Follow Each Other
OnThe Wind Ya' Know
'Cause They Got Nowhere
To Go
That's Why I Want You To
Know

I'm Starting With The Man In
The Mirror
I'm Asking Him To Change
His Ways
And No Message Could Have
Been Any Clearer
If You Wanna Make The World
A Better Place
(If You Wanna Make The
World A Better Place)
Take A Look At Yourself, And
Then Make A Change"

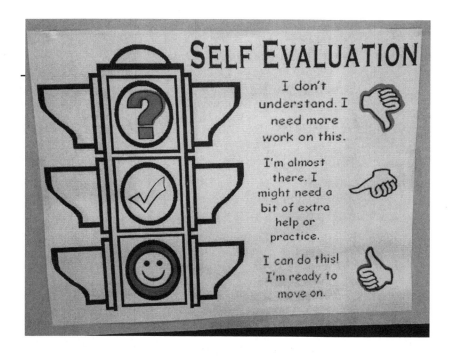

Key Takeaways: A look in the mirror

"Being different starts with how you look at yourself"

If you look in the mirror and see someone who is perfect at everything and has nothing else to learn, you are doomed for eventual failure. Here are some things to think about:

1. **Stagnation is the biggest enemy to long term success.**
   - When things are going well, start working on the next great thing
   - Always look at what is working and what is not.
   - When a concept is doing well, everyone is watching you and will be looking to open up right next to you
   - Your brand gets older every day.

2. **Don't ever take your customers for granted.**
   - The food is a key component of why your customers come in, but that alone will not bring them back

3. **Keep learning. You have not figured everything out yet and never will**
   - You may be good at what you do, but that is not enough for lasting success. Every person and everything around you are a source of education. Become street smart and not just book smart.

4. **Getting better is not the same as being better.**
   - Focus on getting better each and every day. Everyone thinks they are better, but are they really?

5. **Always continue to recognize the people who got you where you are today.**
   - It is very rare when someone became successful on their own. Don't make the mistake of making it about you.

2

WHAT DO YOU WANT TO BE?

As we start on the road to the restaurant business, we all have a different mindset as to where it will lead us. Some people simply work in restaurants to make money as they go through high school and college. Others develop a love for food and want to open up their own restaurant someday. Then there are the people like me, who got the bug as a kid, and became dedicated to the hospitality industry as a career. One thing is very clear about the restaurant business: if you become satisfied and begin to coast, then you will very quickly be out of the business. Therefore, it is no surprise that 59% of restaurants fail in their first three years.

If you are in any way associated with the hospitality industry and have no intention of working hard, then you have picked the wrong industry. Any time you are in the business of making guests happy, you are under the microscope every minute that you are open for business. You can't take your finger off the pulse of the business for a minute. Monday is the same as Saturday night and in fact, it is more important. Busy weekend nights are expected, busy weekday nights are the result of consistent quality food and service.

Today's restaurant industry has more layers than ever before. There is so much more to think about when you make the plunge. Not only that, but as you grow your brand, you need to be constantly adjusting. You must decide if you want to be quick service, fast casual, casual dining or fine dining? Then, you must decide the size of your footprint and where the best real estate is for your brand. Additionally, do you want to be a regional chain, multi concept or have a national presence. From there, it's about determining your customer base and the dayparts you intend to serve. Then, it gets even more involved. Walking traffic, driving traffic, current competition, labor market, parking, construction costs, and more, must be considered. Getting there is very difficult and staying there is more difficult.

It was 1971 and I was 13 years old. It was my first day working at Howdy Beefburger in Quincy, Massachusetts. Howdy Beefburger was launched by Dunkin Donuts founder William Rosenberg. The chain focused on fresh burgers, fresh cut fries, fish sandwiches and shakes. My father was friendly with Bill and decided to open three franchise locations with one of them in Quincy, where the original Dunkin Donuts opened. My first job was putting the pickles on a burger. I then worked my way up to ketchup and mustard and then the buns and finally the burgers. Quality and speed became a focus. I then learned how to make the fries and in general service the customers who came in droves. The most important thing I learned over the next couple years was the preparation that it took to make sure that everyone was ready to service our guests. By the time I was 15, I was running certain shifts and loved every minute of it. I had the bug and it has never left me.

At the time, I had an idea of what I wanted to be, but the picture was fuzzy. The picture has continued to get clearer over the years, but the one thing that has always remained is my dedication to learning new things because perfection can never be reached. Success is built on learning from your successes and failures and by watching and listening to others.

To be in the hospitality industry, you must be able to focus on others. People come to your business for pleasure. Many of your guests work extremely hard and this is their break from reality. They may also be having some tough times in their life or possibly celebrating something. In any case, they are spending valuable money and time with your brand and come to your restaurant with very high expectations. They have so many choices and have chosen you and your business to satisfy them. While you are providing great hospitality and satisfaction to many people, you also are working. All of those weekends where you wanted to be out with friends and family were instead spent making your guests time off special.

When I was working for Hyatt, early in my career, I went through a stretch where I worked 42 days in a row. I still remember the 42 because that time helped me become who I am. When I was transferred to the Hyatt in Cambridge, Massachusetts, my schedule was Tuesday through Sunday with Mondays off. This is when I met my wife, Jayne. Mondays were my Saturdays and I knew very quickly how special she was. We went out every Monday and enjoyed so many great times. Over the years, watching me work hard to build my businesses, she remained amazingly supportive of me and still does.

So, what do you want to be? Not an easy question as it is likely that you have never really posed this question to yourself. Things just happened and you went into a career that has either brought you success, mixed results or failure. So many factors must come together to create successful outcomes, but it still does not answer the question of what do you want to be. The industry will continue to change with or without you. Those that want to reflect on their greatness will in many cases be left in the dust.

Key Takeaways: What do you want to be

"If you become satisfied and begin to coast, you will very quickly find yourself out of the business."

Stay current and understand that you will never fully have a complete grasp of our changing industry. Here are some things to think about:

1. **How did I get into this industry and what has prompted me to make it my career?**
   - When things are going well, start working on the next great thing.
   - Always look at what is working and what is not.
   - When a concept is doing well, everyone is watching you and will be looking to open right next to you.
   - Your brand gets older every day.

2. **What is it about the industry that I like and can I sustain this?**
   - Making my guests happy and wanting more.
   - Building a team that has the same vision that I do.
   - Making a difference in people's lives.

3. **Living with the highs and the lows, and being the one everyone counts on to stay high?**
   - A successful restaurant opening is an incredible high
   - Location closings
   - Weather issues
   - Staffing problems
   - Food cost issues
   - Positive guest feedback

4. **Staying on top of things. How do I remain current?**
   - You are only as good as the experience you provided your guests today
   - Are you paying attention to what is going on in the industry?
   - What are your competitors doing? They are watching you and trying to steal your customers

- Are you operating based upon what has worked in the past

The answer to what you want to be must be answered many times during your career. Clearly big decisions are made early, but the focus on what's next must always be a part of your DNA. By making the adjustments to your original plan, you can stay relevant.

3

HERE COMES THE ICE CREAM MAN

It starts early in your life. You are headed toward life as an entrepreneur where you develop a business plan and work hard to nurture and grow it. An entrepreneur can start their own business as a sole employee or they can build a national brand with a large team. Being an entrepreneur is a mentality and it does not mean that you need to own your own business. Some of the best entrepreneurs, work for entrepreneurs and become part of a great team.

Good entrepreneurs have certain traits that are crucial to success. An entrepreneur is defined as "a person who organizes and operates a business or businesses, taking on greater than normal financial risks to be successful." Being an entrepreneur does not mean that you are a good business person and that you will be successful. You have an idea which you feel is great, and you are willing to take a risk. Now, you have to make it happen. Let's review some of the areas that are constants with a quality entrepreneur.

Vision - An entrepreneur must always have a plan as to where they are and where they want to be. There are numerous bumps in the road and you have to pick yourself up and move forward. You must celebrate your successes and quickly look to what is next. The past, including yesterday, is a learning experience. Entrepreneurs start with an idea and develop a passion to take this idea and make it a reality. One thing that will be evident, early in the process, is that you have deficiencies and it will be crucial to find the right people and products to balance your strengths.

Culture - What you say and what you do become the model for your organization regardless of the size. Leaders who have integrity and are honest will ultimately bring on a team with people who have similar traits. Some lead by example and are not great communicators; however, ultimately the people around you become crucial to carrying on the culture that you have set. Many people feel that culture is overrated while others talk about having a good culture but do not carry it out. I am a big believer in creating a culture that is legitimate, respectful and real.

Team - Great businesses have great teams. A team needs to be balanced. Not everyone is a leader or has an entrepreneurial mentality. Yes, you want people who have the drive that you have and a do what it takes attitude, but having quality, steady team members is equally important. Not everyone wants to knock it out of the park. Some are quite satisfied hitting singles. Entrepreneurs are the company visionaries and their enthusiasm can get contagious in the short term, but in the long term, a team needs direction and great communication.

The ice cream man

When I was a junior in high school, I was given the opportunity to drive an ice cream truck in one of the busiest routes in Massachusetts. My two brothers had been driving this truck prior to me and they had moved on to college. Therefore, it was my turn to take on the business if I wanted it. My brothers made great money operating the business and that intrigued me, but what I learned later was there was more to this than the money. This was a business that required focus.

To get started, I needed to purchase a variety of products to sell. In order to do that, I needed to understand what I was selling and then have the proper inventory to make people happy. I also needed to be aware of outside events that could affect my regular route. I knew my customers were my bread and butter and I could never take them for granted. They were the Monday-Thursday dinner crowd as opposed to weekend guests. This meant I had to be consistent with a focus to be ready to service them with the same passion and purpose for every visit.

I didn't always feel great about the work and at times wanted to be somewhere else. But, I had a responsibility to follow through with what I dedicated myself to. It was so rewarding when I got to my area, rang the bell and watched my clientele line up for service. I was making their day with that popsicle, ice cream sandwich or cannon ball. And I knew that I could never be late. As I moved forward in the restaurant business, I actually came across some of my former customers as guests in my restaurants. It was then that I learned that your actions throughout your life will come back to help you or hurt you later.

So, what is your 'Here comes the ice cream man' story? The itch to become an entrepreneur started somewhere. And it is very important to think back to the times that helped you grow as an individual. Who gave you the opportunity to learn, make mistakes and ultimately make a difference? There is a small percent of the population that had it easy, with their path to success pre-established. However, most of us had to dig deep to get where we are. Sacrifices had to be made and still are being made. Your history tells a story about you, but it is what comes next in your life that will seal the deal. Always look forward to what is next.

Key Takeaways: Here comes the ice cream man

"Being an entrepreneur is a mentality and it does not mean that you have to own your own business."

An entrepreneur thinks a little differently. It is not that you are better at something; rather, that you are thinking about different ways of standing out from the pack. When you do that, you have a better chance of being better.

1. **Certain traits are common among entrepreneurs. They are:**
   - The drive to be creative and get things done at all costs
   - The ability to always look for what is next
   - Being able to turn a dream into a reality
   - Having a love for what they do.
   - The resilience to always get up when they fall

2. **Without these, most entrepreneurs will ultimately fail. Therefore, entrepreneurs need to have:**
   - A long-term vision
   - Integrity
   - Honesty
   - Great Leadership

3. **Great Businesses have great teams.**
   - A successful entrepreneur may not be a great leader, but will hire people who believe in him/her who also are great leaders.
   - Entrepreneurs like other entrepreneurs working for them, but quality, steady team members are crucial to any organization.
   - The employees of a great team enjoy being with each other

4. **How you act throughout your life will have a major effect on your future success.**
   - Every person you interact with in your life could come back to help or haunt you as you move forward.
   - Be respectful of others if you want them to respect you.

- Stay off your high horse! You may be different and more successful than others, but that does not make you better.

Entrepreneurs dig deep to get where they need to go. If they succumb to the lows and dwell on the highs, they may not be an entrepreneur for very long.

4

HAVE A MENTOR AND BE A MENTOR

There is someone or maybe multiple people who want to make a positive impact on your life. It may be a teacher, coach, family friend or a neighbor. What they have in common is that they see something in you. You have potential to stand out in some way and they feel that they can provide you the knowledge, encouragement and support to make a difference in your life. The relationship may be short term or it may be for an extended time, but when you look back, you will remember. You may have created some of your own opportunities by choosing to work while you were going to school. Or in some cases, your parents got you the job. Regardless of how you started, work most likely provided you with spending money and, more important, gave you some clarity on how the business world worked.

Both of my kids, Michael and Amanda, worked in my restaurants during high school and Mike also spent some time working at our corporate office. While they did that, they learned some important things. First and foremost, they decided that they did not want to be in the restaurant business. I had no problem with that. The reason I wanted them to work at the restaurants was not to have them make that a career. What I wanted them to learn was about work ethic, being part of a team, hospitality, and respect for others. To this day, they have used what they learned to have top notch careers in other industries. If you currently do not have interns in both your restaurants and your corporate office, you should rethink your decision. These individuals provide a completely different perspective and are smart and highly focused. They are looking to learn as much as possible and want to be challenged. At the same time, they will question just about everything. If you and your team maintain patience, these interns will have a positive impact on your organization.

As you made important decisions like where to go to college, what career path to take, where to live and work, and so much more, you likely took advice from some people you trusted. While these decisions were ultimately yours to make, these people helped you make those decisions. At work, you also likely watched other people closely and chose a professional mentor who you could model yourself after. This person likely had traits that you respected and who could guide you to move up in your career.

At the same time, as people have guided you in your life, you hopefully have been doing the same for others. That also starts early and you may not have even known that you were having a major impact on someone else. Have you ever coached sports or had younger teammates? What about tutoring younger kids in school or training others at a job? I am sure you took a liking to other people and helped them in many ways. You saw something and felt you could make an impact on them.

I remember my first job out of college. I graduated from Cornell and was ready to begin my career in the hotel business. I took a job with Hyatt Hotels and where did they send me? Los Angeles! Here I was, at 20 years old, a kid from Boston who went to school in New York, and I was off to the other side of the country not knowing a soul. All I knew was that I would be working for a former graduate of Cornell, Norm Rich. I was happy about that, but really did not understand what that meant at the time. He had a high-level position at the hotel and beyond meeting me, I did not expect to get much of his time. I assure you, he did not make it easy for me. In fact, I worked my butt off. At one point, I worked forty-two days in a row (yes, I remember how many days in a row). But I was learning and being given responsibility and he was meeting with me weekly to teach me and push me to be great at what I did. He had plans for me. I just did not know what, where or when.

Less than a year after I started, I was promoted and moved to another hotel in LA where I was working for another Cornell grad, John Banta. The pattern continued and I moved from hotel to hotel and Cornell grad to Cornell grad. I was sent to premium locations where I would be given the opportunity to excel. They were my mentors, but it was still up to me to work hard and get results. I was given the opportunity and I didn't disappoint them. I was not better than anyone else, but I was different. They saw that in me and gave me the chance to stand out.

Throughout my career I have remembered what I have learned from others and the confidence they put in me. I have mentored so many people over the years and continue to take pride in this. Yes, I spend time with current and former Cornell students. I am sure to speak at classes every year. I also spend time with newer professors to help them understand the future of our industry. I also work closely with my team to help them both professionally and personally, and do everything I can to take calls and meet with industry professionals who are looking to share their new ideas with me. I don't have all the answers, but I have opinions and knowledge that I want to share. The best part of being a mentor to others is what you learn from them. I love learning and everyone has something to share that I have not learned or have not figured out. Everyone is so busy in today's world, but I will never understand why a seasoned professional would not respond to a person seeking advice. Furthermore, I see it as such a sign of disrespect to not respond to another professional who has reached out in an effort to learn new ideas. My emails and texts are very short and to the point. Part of the reason is that I try to respond to everyone who should get a response.

My advice is to give back! You can make a difference. Share your successes and make an impact on others. Giving to charities is nice, but helping people in the hospitality industry and in your daily life is special. You will feel rewarded in ways that are unimaginable.

Hyatt LAX 1980- Where it all began

Hyatt HILTON HEAD ISLAND 1984- My last
hotel before moving to restaurants

Key Takeaways: Have a mentor and be a mentor

"Who along the way saw the potential in you and helped you become who you are today?" Yes, there was hard work and you focus on the path that made you successful, but along the way, someone was guiding you.

At the same time, what impact have you had on others. You have a lot to share with rising stars in our industry. They have hidden talents that are not being used and they have egos that need to be kept in check. You can influence what they become.

Here is your assignment:

1. <u>Who had an influence on who you are today in your career?</u>
   A.
   B.
   C.

2. <u>What key things did you learn along the way that had an impact on your career?</u>
   A.
   B.
   C.

3. <u>Name some people in the industry that you helped guide to be successful in the industry (Not training, but mentorship)</u>
   A.
   B.
   C.

The people that you mentor have all provided you with an education. Everyone has qualities that they can share. It is up to you to keep learning so we can continue to improve who we are.

5

WHAT DO YOU SEE?

I remember my first day as a restaurant manager at TJ Peppercorns at the Hyatt LA Airport. My boss, the general manager, asked me a simple question as we entered the restaurant: 'What do I see?' I wanted to make a great impression, but I really did not know how to answer the question. I figured it would safe to answer in a very general way, which was to talk about what the staff was doing to prepare for opening and I said that in general the restaurant looked great. His comment to me was, "Now that you are done kissing my butt, tell me what you really see!" As a young, 20-year-old manager, who just moved across the country, I was a little nervous after that and I was wondering, what did I get myself into?

He made it clear to me that day that we were on the same team. We were about taking care of our guests and having them come back as frequently as possible. In order to do that, we needed to make sure that our thoughts and feelings were kept in check because our guests really did not care about them. I understood at that point, that there were high expectations. I also understood that he was going to give me direction to make me a successful manager, and to make him more successful as my boss.

After our initial conversation, he showed me what he saw: a light bulb that was burned out from across the room, a picture that was hanging a little crooked and an employee's shirt that was wrinkled and therefore unable to work that day. He gave me a pad of paper and a pen and told me to spend the next 30 minutes writing down 100 things that I saw, starting with the outside of the building and then throughout the restaurant itself. I really had to focus and I did find quite a few things, but not 100. He told me that ultimately, I would come to see a lot more than I did today and not only that, I would see these things from one spot. Eventually, he said, it would just come natural to me. And it did. Immediately upon entering a room I would see a crooked picture or a burned out light bulb, salt and pepper shakers that were not full as well as them being on a table backwards (Salt should be on the left).

To help me along, he gave me a laminated two-sided card that fit into my shirt pocket. It was a checklist of what to look for and he said that after 30 days I would not need it anymore. He was right! What I saw each day became a critical part of who I was and still makes up who I am today. It taught me about focus and attention to detail. I have used it with my teams and for many of them, it changed the way they look at things. You can always point things out to others, but the best way to learn is on your own. Everyone can learn so much just by standing in one spot and simply taking it all in. I used to seek out certain spots in the restaurants that were the best places to see more things. In some cases, I had to sit at a table to get a different perspective. Can you really see debris under tables by standing? The point of view from being low is a totally different perspective from one that is high. I used to sit with my managers at very specific tables and asked, "What do you see?"

So, this is really about the little things that differentiate you from the pack. In most cases, a flaw in something that you deem small, can offset everything that you did well. How many times have you been to a restaurant where you had a great meal yet they gave you poor quality coffee at the end? Have you been to a restaurant with great food, but the bread basket is ordinary? What about a five-star hotel that has all the bells and whistles, but the toilet paper in the restroom was like sandpaper? It is also important to remember that your guests see things also. If there is a view into the kitchen and they see sloppiness, they will make assumptions that their food will not be great. If they use the restroom and it is a mess or the paper towels are empty, it will reflect how they feel about the restaurant. If they see an employee who is not practicing proper sanitary practices, they will assume that this is how you operate your brand. Attention to detail is what you and your staff need to catch early and often before your guests, customers or clients see it first.

And this requires training. Your entire staff needs to be trained on attention to detail and they need to be rewarded for being the guardians of your business. I have always used a certification process for both managers and staff. It became almost a club focused on standards. Anyone who was certified was rewarded with certain benefits. Those team members who became certified trainers were rewarded further and many of them ultimately became store opening trainers, supervisors and managers. Your facility, including the rest rooms, must match the standard that you have set. The overall experience is what brings guests back. The food always seems to taste better when all of the other components of the experience are great.

It really all starts with what you see. I can't think of a time where I did not bring a manager or team member to one of those key spots and asked them: "What do you see?" The truth is that nothing is ever perfect and we need others to give us the feedback. We need to strive for perfection. Success takes a long time to achieve and failure can happen very quickly. Never stop looking because others are always watching.

The view from my table.

Another view: You can't see it unless you are sitting

Key Takeaways: What do you see?

"Sometimes the leader chooses not to see things and wants to believe that everything is perfect around them. Nothing is ever perfect and we need others to give us the feedback. We need to strive for perfection."

1. **It is about the guest/customer/client and not about you.**

- We may think we are better than our competition, but we are not the ones making the decision on where they will spend their money.
- We must seek out feedback from our customers and not take what they say personally. We must use it to make us improve.

2. **Details are what makes you different from the rest of the pack.**

- Focus on the little things.
- Do something that creates a buzz.
- Make sure your guests always feel good about your experience.

3. **Train yourself and others to get better.**

- Create tools that will motivate your team to want to understand how to better themselves.
- Develop a "what do you see program" and make it part of your culture. More than that, make it fun.

4. **It is about the overall experience and each of us have different expectations.**

- Don't assume that everyone is looking for the same experience when they come into your restaurants.
- Give them something to talk about when they leave.

Ordinary will lead to eventual failure. Extraordinary will lead to continued success.

6

ASK LOTS OF QUESTIONS

Most of us, have a tendency, to come up with solutions before we know what the problem is. I don't know about you, but when I go to the doctor for my yearly physical, the doctor asks me how I am feeling and then does a series of tests. He does not say hello and then tell me that I have a cold, give me my medicine and send me on my way. A doctor will continue to ask questions to diagnose a problem. If you have a sore shoulder, the doctor needs to understand how the injury occurred, how long it has been sore and where exactly does it hurt. Very few things are black and white.

When you are in the hospitality business, there are many people who work for you that have a much better understanding of what is going on in their world than you do. You are the ultimate decision maker and must hold your team to execute a plan, but the plan should come from the findings from your guests and team. It is beautiful that you, on your own, do not have to come up with all the answers. By encouraging others to provide their thoughts, and feedback you will be much better equipped to work on customized solutions to each obstacle that you may face.

I have always been a person of structure. A day in the restaurant business should be as scripted as much as possible, so you can provide your guests with the experience they are paying for. This means that you must be ready when the guests arrive. This involves proper purchasing with accurate par levels. It involves proper receiving and storage so that you are maximizing your yields and shelf life. Detailed production sheets with accurate par levels, and on and on it goes. Every day in the restaurant business is an adventure and there will be things that come up that are not expected. But being ready makes it that much easier to be nimble.

I spent a lot of time over the years both in the hotel and restaurant business talking to my guests. I asked lots of questions so I could find out what they liked and what they didn't like. I never went to a table and said how is your meal? What kind of an answer am I going to get with a question like that? Good or bad! It is important to never ask a yes or no question. It tells you nothing. Better questions would be: 'What was your favorite part of dinner tonight? I noticed you had our burger. It is a new blend with ground short rib. How did you like it?' Or, 'I hope you enjoyed the turkey tips. We are continuing to work on healthier options and that dish has only 600 calories.' The point is that I cared about what the guest thought. I was not always going to like what I heard, but I needed their feedback to do a better job.

I also counted on my servers, cashiers and other employees to tell me what was really going on with our guests. In effect, they were our sales people and had the most contact with our customers. What types of questions were our guests asking? What positive and negative feedback were they hearing? I also encouraged bus staff and dishwashers to point out what was not being eaten or being thrown in the trash. Maybe there was too much food or possibly an item that was consistently not being eaten. You spend so much time developing food, costing it out and then coming up with a sell price so you can make a profit. Imagine serving a pasta dish with a breadstick that costs you 20 cents and finding that 80% of the time, the breadstick is not being eaten.

My brother Larry and I spent years growing Fresh City and Souper Salad. Both concepts were developed to be fast casual before fast casual existed. We understood that quality needed to be executed in a fast environment. We also understood that our guests wanted what they wanted, and they wanted it fast. Therefore, we were constantly adjusting to the flow of the restaurants and to anything else that made the guest experience better.

I spent a lot of time behind the line with our employees during peak lunch periods. The time for me to be in the restaurants was when we were busiest. I could interact with staff and customers, but I also could see what was working and what wasn't. This mindset never changed as our companies grew. I watched for bottlenecks that caused delays in execution. Was the line stocked, was a team member slow, inefficient or not trained well? Despite it being busy, was the team communicating with excitement to our customers? One of my biggest concerns was how long it took for the last person in line to order and get their food. If we could not get this done in a proper amount of time, they would leave and go somewhere else. To help with this concern, we set up express lines specific to certain items. Our brands were focused on customization, but customization can take time. Those that wanted quality and speed could get stir fry with our stock vegetables rather than pick their own. The same held true for our wraps, salads, burritos and sandwiches. Play to the crowd and find out what their goal is. They are not all the same and my focus was to take care of all of them. To do that, I needed to be creative. They only way to do that was to spend time with my team in the trenches to see how they interacted with our guests and where the roadblocks were.

Never take your team for granted. They are the ones with the answers and they have a tremendous bearing on your success or failure. Ask them lots of questions on how they feel execution can improve the experience of the guests. It is your call on the ultimate plan, but be sure to ask lots of questions of others before you tell everyone the answers.

Key Takeaways: Ask Lots of Questions

"When you are in the hospitality business, there are many people who work for you that have a much better understanding of what is going on in their world than you do."

1. <u>**Talk to your guests and ask them questions that have meaning.**</u>

- 'How is everything?' is very broad and will give you only broad answers.

- Be as specific as possible. You want your guests to be honest and provide you with information to help you get better.

- Find out how they make their choice of coming to your restaurants vs somewhere else. Social media and surveys can tell you some things, but talking to people face-to-face can tell you more.

2. <u>**What is really going on in your restaurants?**</u>

- Talk to your staff. They are the ones that interact with your guests.

- Your staff knows what the guests are requesting and where you are falling short.

- Are the systems you put in place working? It is quite possible that these systems are causing service to be slow and not your staff.

3. <u>**What does your guest really want?**</u>

- What do they consider to be value?

- How important is speed of service?

- What are your competitors doing that your guests prefer?

- Where does customization fall in terms of priorities?

"Never take your team for granted. They are the ones with the answers and they have a tremendous bearing on your success or failure."

7

WALKABOUTS

You have a great location in a high traffic area. You have quite a bit of competition; however, you are positioned to do more than your share. Unfortunately, people are either walking or driving by your location, but it is not necessarily to eat at a competitor. What is going on? The assumption here is that you are doing something wrong or maybe there is a new business taking away from yours. In truth, there are so many variables that may affect your business that you would not be able to understand from your desk.

Let me tell you a story about Filene's Basement, a Boston institution that opened in 1908. It was considered to be the first discount priced store in history. The store was created, originally, to sell excess clothing from the department store above. As Filene's Basement became a destination, it started to sell top line brands at a discount. In fact, some of the finest designer brands had special sales at Filene's Basement, which was a draw for Boston's business community. Filene's Basement also had big wedding dress events, among other special sales, and automatic price reductions week by week. The store was a tremendous draw for the Boston Financial District crowd, who would walk to "the basement" to see if the particular clothes they had been watching were still there at a lower price. You had the potential of getting a tremendous deal by waiting or possibly finding out that the item you wanted was gone. The problem for Souper Salad was that people were spending their lunch hour shopping instead of eating.

The key at this stage was understanding what the problem was and then coming up with the solution. Souper Salad, at that time, focused in on a bottomless salad bar, homemade soups and sandwiches. We knew that we could not get all of these people to change their mindset of shopping over eating, yet we knew they were likely hungry. So, we tried to figure out how we could get our customers to eat while they were walking to shop.

This was not a problem that had an easy answer, and reacting quickly would only cause more chaos. For us, it was all about figuring out where the opportunities were to solve the problem and then coming up with a strategy that could ultimately lead to increased sales and goodwill. The one thing that was crystal clear, was that: these people were eating. They were either bringing lunch from home, picking it up or having it delivered so they could eat at their desk while working and spend their lunch hour shopping.

After a great deal of testing and marketing, the Walkabout was born. It featured a variety of salads wrapped tightly in fresh pita bread, which was secured by foil. It did not leak and it was easy to walk with as you peeled it down. Most of all, every bite tasted great and it was healthier than most products available at the time. Over the years, hundreds of varieties were created, but there were always 12 available. It was a product that was never duplicated and ended up being a winner for both the operator and customer.

And it worked because it was simply different. You must re-invent constantly and look for the next challenge. The customer is looking for great food and service, which is a given, but that is not enough to sustain and grow your business. The needs of the consumer continue to change. Maybe you do not have customers who have moved away from eating to go shopping, but there are other challenges that you face that you must react to. We all have dealt with changing traffic patterns, construction, the closing of a store that provided you with a lot of your business, and of course competition. They all start out as obstacles, but become great opportunities and challenges. If you react to an opportunity in a positive and focused way, you will find solutions.

At one time, there were no drive thru in restaurants. Customers used to go in and either wait for a fresh product or they received a pre-made product so the people could be serviced quickly. McDonalds, for many years, did just that. Making something customized was unusual and not something they really wanted to do. Pre-made items went away over time and customization became the norm. With the advent of customization, service efficiencies were introduced primarily with drive-thru.

The first thing that needs to be done is to observe your operations and see where the bottlenecks are. It could be the layout of your restaurant, service system, productivity of staff, execution of food that is too complex, and so much more. Once the observations have been done, you need to come up with where the opportunities are to improve and prioritize, which will ultimately give you the quickest and most positive results. These results need to make your guests happier and lead to a better bottom line. Finally, you need to develop the solutions, and that is what the Walkabout was for Souper Salad. It solved a problem for that one location, but the product itself was so good that it became one of the top selling items for the entire company. And ultimately, we made it a staple item at Fresh City.

Your brand encounters obstacles all the time. Some are regional and some are national. Just like any limited time offer, solutions need to be well thought-out and tested methodically. This solution may still get rolled out regionally or nationally or it may not be rolled out at all if it really is not a solution. The Walkabout worked out in every way. There were hundreds of other so-called solutions that never worked. There is a special thing about the restaurant business. It allows you to get knocked down and get up quickly to work on the next great thing. It is what makes our business so unique.

The Walkabout: Individual or Catering

FILENES BASEMENT- Walkabouts solved the problem!!!

Key Takeaways: Walkabouts

"People are either walking or driving by your location, but it is not necessarily to go eat at your competitor. What is going on?"

Sometimes you really don't know, but you need to dig deep and figure out what the problem is and focus in on potential solutions.

1. **Understand what the problem is.**
    - Don't make assumptions.
    - Follow the pattern. Is it the menu mix changing, or is it certain day parts or times that are affected?
    - Ask questions of your team, customers and retail neighbors

2. **Address your problem methodically and not with a quick reaction.**
    - Take a deep dive into what the problem is and how it started.
    - Is this a short term or long-term problem?
    - Is this an easy solution or one that is complex?

3. **Problems become opportunities and opportunities lead to winning solutions**
    - Solving problems can be extremely exciting. It is a challenge that you want to win.
    - Bring your team in on possible solutions. You need creativity if you want to be offensive vs defensive.
    - Talk to your customers about what would make them over the top happy.

Be proactive about everything you do. There are many things that will continue to change the industry and your business, and if you and your team stay focused on what is happening around you, your brand will stay current.

8

EMOTIONAL VS NON-EMOTIONAL

How many decisions do you make that are strictly based on emotion? I will tell you, it is probably a lot more than you think.

None of us really believe that we make emotional decisions. What we do know is that we are successful at most things we do. We tend to assume that the decisions we make are what any other smart individual would make. In truth, we make emotional decisions all the time and many of those decisions are costing you money.

Any time I mention emotional vs non-emotional decisions, people seem confused and say: "I never heard anyone describe decision making in that way." However, we all frequently make emotional decisions. In many cases, it's for all the wrong reasons. This applies as much to our business as it does to our personal lives.

So, what is an emotional decision and where does it fit into your business?

How about when you are selling fish and chips in your restaurants. You are taking a white fish and using a delicious beer batter. You insist that you will only use cod for your fish n' chips. But the fact is that nowhere on your menu does it say cod. I guarantee that if I did a blind tasting for you and your guests and used a swai or pollock instead, no one would notice the difference. Furthermore, you could keep your price on the menu the same and lower your food cost. If you decide to list cod as the fish being used for your fish and chips, you are setting yourself up for large fluctuations in food cost because cod prices are extremely variable. It also gives you no flexibility to change your fish. It is so amazing that decisions like this take place all the time by very smart people.

What about this one? You use a tremendous amount of produce in your operations and have been using the same produce distributor since you opened your first location. Yet, after taking a hard look at their pricing and quality level, they are grossly over charging you and the quality is nothing special, but they were with you at the beginning? Sometimes an operator fails to remember that these long-term relationships cost a ton of money to their business. And there are a couple reasons for this.

First, everyone will look out for themselves before they look out for you. Second place is never bad, but first place is much better. Second, when you have a long-term relationship, you will take your eye off what you are being sold. You trust the people and honestly, they are not trying to over-charge you. But they are secure in the relationship so they take their eye off things, too. The distributor tends to focus on the customers who are challenging their every move and not one that is loyal and trusts them unconditionally. What is even more incredible is that I have seen many instances where an operator is so loyal to that distributor that they will continue to overpay.

I hear many times that a certain distributor or consultant saved the brand a lot of money early in the growth of the company or when times were tough and business was off, they extended your terms. I commend these companies and people for being loyal to you and supporting you along the way. I also want to make it clear that they were making money while all of this was going on. Your loyalty is important and I appreciate the fact that you remember, but it does not have to be for life. There are many other people and companies who could have done the same thing for you and it was simply timing, which was the key cog. If another distributor, consultant or person can do more for you today, I would recommend that you listen. If you were the coach of a football team that had won many championships with a quarterback that you drafted, coached and won with, would you replace him with another quarterback if he lost his skills. Or, would you keep him playing and begin to lose? Keeping the diminished skilled quarterback playing would be an emotional decision leading to inferior results.

Are you getting credit?

You have put your heart and soul into your brand and have focused on the fact that you go above and beyond with the quality of your food. You are making your soups from scratch, baking in-house and doing so much more. It drives you insane that your main competitor is not going to the same lengths that you are and yet some of your guests tell you that they like their soups better than yours. How can this be possible? You try to tell your guests about the differences, but in the end, they don't care. The emotional operator will dig in their heels and simply say that their soups are better. The non-emotional operator will evaluate the situation and focus in on what the problem is. Even though my soups are made from scratch, are they as consistent as the ones my competitor is buying? Do they taste as good? Do they look as good? Have I done blind tastings of my soups vs the competition and discovered the difference? Or, do I need some neutral tasters who have no skin in the game?

After going through a series of due diligence, you can then understand that maybe some of your scratch soups are not that good while some are excellent. Maybe you realized you don't have to make all your soups in house. If you want to provide your guests with the best of the best, buy the best stock soups and then doctor them up to make them homemade. Yes, buy a great chicken soup and add fresh chicken or southwest seasonings to raise the bar.

Different remains the focus. We all think we are better, but that decision belongs to the consumer, who is paying for the products in your restaurants.

Doing an emotional vs non-emotional exercise will be very helpful to you and your organization. You also want to redo the exercise periodically. It is a very simple question that takes a great deal of thought. Besides yourself, I would have as many management people do it as well and make it anonymous through a survey. Many of your team know how passionate you are about certain things and would be afraid to speak up. You can take the results and come up with your short list of non-negotiables and then begin working on potential adjustments for everything else.

A delicious fresh broth which is customized at each restaurant

Key Takeaways: Emotional vs Non-Emotional

"You are making many decisions every day that are based on emotion. Many of these decisions are costing you a great deal of money"

We deal with the assumption that our customers and staff think the same way we do. The truth is that they don't at all.

1. **<u>What is an emotional decision?</u>**

- One that doesn't factor in what is best for you and your business.
- One that is tied to old relationships and keeping things status quo.
- One that involves payback for something that was done when you needed help.
- One that you think is good for your business, but is not.

2. **<u>Why do you make emotional decisions?</u>**

- Ego
- Having lost sight of what is really going on in your business.
- Too many ties to memory lane. Not focused on reality.
- Not communicating with your team or guests.

3. **<u>Are you always getting credit for what you do?</u>**

- Take a look at your competitors and what they are doing well.
- Talk to your guests and employees to get their opinions.
- Do lots of blind tastings and do them frequently.

4. **<u>How can you become less emotional in your decision making?</u>**

- Look at your sales and profit and think about whether you can improve each if you look at things differently.
- Understand that some of your old relationships, including friends and family, are costing you money. It is nothing malicious, but you are taking your eye off the ball.

When you make decisions, be sure to look to others for input. You are the final decision maker, but ego should not be a factor when making an emotional decision.

PART TWO:

—

WHERE AM I GOING?

9

YOU ARE BEING WATCHED

A smart business person is constantly watching everything and never takes for granted that they have it all figured out. If you are in the restaurant business, like I am, we know that we have an important responsibility to make our guests happy. At the same time, we must be realistic. We are not working on a cure for a deadly disease.

The fact is that scientists have breakthroughs all the time and those lead to the next discovery. They have a quick celebration and then they move on to what is next. These scientists also want to stay relevant and they know that there are many others trying to discover the same thing. Many of those scientists will collaborate for the good of society, while others are more focused on being the one who finds the cure.

So, what does this have to do with you and the restaurant business? If you have restaurants that are busy, you are being watched. It could be current competitors or potential competitors looking for locations. They are coming in to try your food and go through the service system. They are sitting in your dining rooms in places where they can eat, see what is going on and hear customers. They watch your deliveries in the morning to understand who your vendors are. They are even trying to take pictures if you allow them to. Whatever you are doing well, they will try to mimic it and then make it better. They may then do it at a discount to drive customers away from you and to them. Without question, they will try to steal some of your management and employees because they know some of the magic potion. This is when you will know if your team is loyal to you and your company or loyal strictly to make more money.

At this stage, you are feeling good about yourself. You are busy and turning a profit. Now let's say that you are written up in a restaurant publication or even better, given an award by the industry. You now have companies trying to purchase you or private equity trying to invest. You attend conferences and are asked to speak and everyone wants to discuss your magic potion for success. You love the attention, but are you taking your eye off your business? You are now not only being watched, you are being studied. There will be copy cats throughout the country trying to take what you have and make the food better and the service faster. They will look at your design and general footprint and use it to help them. Finally, they will be visiting your restaurants and watching! What is crucial is to always be ahead of the game: working on innovation six months to a year in advance. By understanding the trends early, you can work on new things, conduct tests and then implement those innovations before anyone else. You want to remain the brand that is cutting edge.

I don't want to make it seem like success is a bad thing. It is really the opposite, but if you do not prepare for success and ultimately use it as a springboard for more success, you will fail. We see it all the time. You want to grow fast because you are hot, but you grow too fast and can't control the quality of the food and service that you started with. The numbers begin to fall and you slowly are not the toast of the town anymore. Change can be extremely difficult when your brand becomes bigger and you are under pressure to open locations. However, without quality changes, you can easily lose momentum. A certain part of your menu should be adjusted every six months for innovative products. That means that some products will need to be removed from the menu. Your customers will appreciate your focus on being current. Ride the wave of success and do it in the same way that got you there in the first place. This means to never take your eye off your business.

So, what does this have to do with you and how you are perceived as a person? From early on in your life, you were being watched by the people around you. They looked at who you spent time with and how you treated other people. They also observed whether you were a leader or a follower. Are you looking at how you can get better or are you satisfied with where you are? The pattern of being observed continues throughout your life, whether in good times or bad ones. People are watching and evaluating you. The people that you bullied, snubbed or had an attitude with could easily be the people you need later. How you come across at a conference or local event can define you. People remember when they have been snubbed as they move up in the industry. They will always take note of how they remember you. Some of these people could have the real estate or money you need to grow. Others could be manufacturers who have a strong supply of product that your current vendor doesn't.

Let me tell you about my experience of being watched. Believe me, I went through the phases of concept development, spending time in the lines at the restaurants, flattering articles, speaking at conferences, and winning industry awards. The one thing that stands out is that our team remained part of everything from beginning to end. My brother Larry and I did not do this on our own. We needed a great team to make our concept great and to keep it there. The articles written were about the whole team and when Fresh City won the Nation's Restaurant News Hot Concept Award in 2002, the recognition went to our entire team. In fact, when we accepted the award, there were quite a few people from our team there with us. To this day, I never take anything for granted and I focus on the people who I work with as well as the people in the industry who I respect and admire. And the ones who I don't respect and admire, I ignore, because like many, I have an excellent memory.

You never know who is watching. They could have an impact on your success. Treat people with respect and they will do the same.

Key Takeaways: You are being watched

"If you are having any level of success in the restaurant business, then you are being watched closely by people who want to meet or exceed your level of success."

You are also being watched as to how you handle success. Are you full of yourself or have you remained true to who you were when you were on the way up?

1. **Success is a process.**
- Understand that you did not get there on your own.
- Stick to your core roots. Never forget where you came from.
- Keep your foot on the gas, otherwise your success will fade.

2. **How are you perceived in your business?**
- People will try to copy you, but your focus should always be to stay one step ahead.
- Create a great culture. People may leave you to start their own companies, but their respect for you in the industry is key.
- Everything is not a competition. Stay professional.

3. **How are you perceived as a person?**
- The value of your reputation can be crucial to your success in business.
- Be respectful of people on the way up. That was you at one time.
- Treat manufacturers, distributors and others in the industry with class and dignity. You may be a great negotiator, but do it right.

"Being watched means that you need to be on your game at all times. A true industry leader wants to be challenged."

10

TAKE THE PATH TOWARD IMPROVEMENT

There are so many people in world who think they know everything and are better than everyone else at almost everything they do. Reality says that beyond a few things, being the best is subjective. It is usually ego driven and most often detrimental to your success. Confidence, on the other hand, is crucial to success. We should all feel that we have the tools to be the best at anything. The key is to understand that everything is a journey and will not come easy. Sometimes we wake up and go on the scale and see that we gained a few pounds. You then come to realize that you have not been eating as well as normal and have been skipping going to the gym. No problem, you are going to spend the next 30 days eating better and going back to the gym. You look at your calendar for the next month and there is a lot of travel and you are entertaining people. How are you going to stick to your plan? For me, staying busy was always my best diet. I always did a lot of tasting and eating in moderation when I had my restaurants and I was very active physically. I went to the gym at set times every week. I actually scheduled the gym on my calendar. Just like anything, the journey to improve must be well planned and calculated. Nothing comes easy.

The restaurant industry has a lot of art associated with it. From the food to restaurant design and plate presentations. Artists are creative and they tend to be single-minded on themselves and what they can create. They may appreciate what other artists do, but for the most part, they feel their art is the best. Unfortunately, the restaurant business is team oriented and the single-minded approach generally will not work. If you are bigger than everyone else and the perception of your team is that they are inferior to you, then you will not get maximum productivity or may ultimately lose them to a competitor.

My approach has always been to hire people who are better than me at their area of expertise. The only thing I needed to be the best at was managing my team and maximizing their productivity. I had to always be challenging myself and my team so we could be focused on getting better. I wanted them to think as a team. I trained them always to be part of a chain of dots. The goal of the organization was always to connect the dots and if they did not do their part, it would bring down everyone else on the team. Pride is always a major factor in performance once you get by salary.

When I was starting to grow brands, I was very protective of them and did not want to share what I was doing, but what was I really hiding? I was clearly hiding some of my flaws and did not really know it. Who, but another top-notch restauranteur would see things in a different way than I did. The truth of the matter is when you walk through your restaurants you begin to not see things in the same way. You may be a bit brainwashed that everything is perfect or at least close to perfect. When you go to a competitor or another restaurant you are extremely critical of everything. You see all the flaws because you go in with an open mind and are really looking for flaws. Looking at your own restaurants in a more critical way can bring out some opportunities to improve your business.

When my brother and I sold our company, we both went into different areas of consulting to help support our industry colleagues. I know that I had a wealth of knowledge in the industry, but more so I had an open mind and would be able to make observations which would result in opportunities. I would not be looking for flaws, I would be looking for opportunities. The issues I faced surprised me. First, some operators did not want me to see what was going on because I was going to see the "secret sauce". Second, when I did come in and observe and present the opportunities, these operators were defensive. This told me they were on a path to stagnation, which is dangerous.

There were also a couple other big surprises. One was that purchasing executives were afraid of anyone seeing opportunities as it would make them look bad. I could never understand that, as no one is great at everything, including purchasing execs. But, more of a surprise were the multi-unit executives who knew that they needed support, but then backed off because someone from their team said, 'we don't need any outsider coming in here.' Everyone today is chef driven, which creates a very unclear term. Any restaurant that has a head chef uses the term but food alone does not make a great brand, and in many cases, chef-driven means inconsistent quality from location to location.

As a consultant, I never failed to save a company money. I can also tell you stories of savings opportunities up to seven figures that were passed on because someone did not want to hurt someone else's feelings. In an industry of small bottom lines, being open-minded could be the difference between thriving or dying. I always wondered why restaurant executives would not want to save money if their quality was maintained or improved. I also found it confusing how a purchasing executive who is being paid to save their company money, could knowingly turn down the opportunity to do just that because they were worried about getting credit.

There are so many areas to improve on both personally and professionally. The path to improvement starts with having an open-mind and the desire to get better. Protect what you feel is necessary, but for the most part, look at everyone and everything having to do with your business. Seek out the endless possibilities that exist to improve your business. Recognize what you are good at and what each member of your team is good at and then seek outside support to balance it all. Learn to trust your partners. They are all accountable to provide results and that is how they will be judged.

Taking a Path to Improvement. There always is a better way!

Key Takeaways: Taking the path to improvement

"There are many people in key industry positions who think they are experts in everything. Nobody is an expert in everything and in fact you can count on one hand the number of people in the world who are actually proven to be the very best at anything"

Surround yourself with great people and recognize them for being part of your success.

1. **Have an open mind. You and your brand can improve every day.**
   - Listen to your team.
   - Listen to your guests/customers/clients.
   - Stay tuned-in to what is going on around you and in the industry. Don't let time pass you by.

2. **Be protective of your brand, but not to a fault.**
   - You should protect your brand and be proud of what you have accomplished, but it is far from perfect.
   - Don't discount the good things that your competitors are doing.
   - Watch for signs that business is going somewhere else.

3. **Hire people that are better than you in their area of expertise.**
   - Surround yourself with great people.
   - Recognize their strengths and learn from them.
   - Manage these strengths to provide your guests/customers/clients with a great experience/partnership.

4. **Having a professional "partner" take a look at things from the outside will have a positive impact on your business.**
   - Don't hide your flaws.
   - A professional partner has no interest in stealing your "secret sauce."
   - You will learn a great deal from an outside point of view and will be able to react quickly to the opportunities.

Confidence is extremely important to be successful. Drive and determination make your chances even greater, but humility is one of those things that is a given if you want to be a true leader.

11

NO TIME TO SAVE MONEY

One of the biggest obstacles to running a great business is lack of time. All multi-unit restaurant brands start out with one location and grow from there. Most of these brands have an entrepreneur who founded the brand and worked extremely hard to make it successful. To do that, they needed to wear many hats and prioritize their responsibilities. They clearly had to drive revenue, but they also had to be extremely conscious of cost.

Early on, you had to fight for every penny. You did whatever you had to do, such as physically working in each position as needed, communicating with your guests and purchasing your products by bidding out everything. You were tough. An incredible negotiator. Everyone was supposedly fighting for your business and you were beating them up to the last penny. In your mind, you had the best prices in the city and the amount of time you spent was well worth it.

Gradually you begin to get busier. You now needed to look at real estate for new locations and you found yourself focused on many other areas having to do with growth. In addition to the purchasing of food and related items, you now were bidding on your construction, real estate, and so many more areas. There was simply not enough time to do things and you did not have the infrastructure to handle everything. You begin to delegate tasks to other people who did not have the skills. They were able to learn from you and "muscle it," but ultimately your costs start to rise. You also started to rely on non-company people to help you make decisions. This could be distributors, manufacturers, brokers, and others, who may also have become friends of yours. Ultimately, they are first focused on making money for their company and themselves, and then you. You are therefore relying on them because you do not have enough time to do it yourself and you trust them as your friends.

This story is consistent, whether you are growing from 1-2 locations or 5-10, 10-20, 50-100, and so on. All restaurant brands are in transition no matter what the size, and many of the people within the organization are wearing many hats. While they are doing a fabulous job at 50% of what they do, they are doing a mediocre job at the other half. We all have a bucket of cash and try not to spend more than what is in the bucket. In the restaurant business, we need to spend the cash first on what the guest sees and experiences, so that would-be operations. The support team, whether it is supply chain, marketing, HR, or Finance and Administration, would have to wait. In most cases, they are shorthanded and doing too much. If you spend more than what is in the bucket, which many growing companies do, you are rolling the dice. Eventually, you will have to go back to running financials that are viable for you and whoever it is that you may be accountable to, including investors, banks, private equity and any other "partners".

After Fresh City won the Hot Concepts award from Restaurant News, I got extremely busy. There was a lot that needed to be done and clearly my brother and I needed to work on a variety of new and exciting things to support our growth. I was personally very stretched for a time. I was now dealing with licensing deals, franchise deals and suddenly, had locations in six states. I did make some unfortunate mistakes, such as relying on some outside people to help me save money. In some cases, I became friendly with some of my vendors and trusted them to do the right thing. For the most part, they came through and they remained my partners and in others they took advantage of me. Over time, you learn about who are stand up people and who are not and you make adjustments both in your business and your personal life. It is a small world and you never know when you will cross paths again.

I chalk it up to continued learning as you grow and making mistakes as part of it.

As I moved away from starting and running restaurant brands, I began to partner with multi-unit brands on cost reduction without sacrificing quality. Sounds like a no-brainer when you can save money without sacrificing quality, but it isn't. There were so many times that I showed six and even seven figure savings to operators and they said, "I am too busy to look at this now, maybe another time." When I heard this, it blew my mind. Too busy to save money? I tried to understand. What were these people doing that made them so busy? I still deal with these types of clients today, but I now ask lots of questions to try to get some clarity.

Why would someone be too busy to save money? I had a casino out in Vegas that I was working on a produce management program for. Their volume was staggering and their relationship went back many years. My analysis showed $1 Million in savings per year with quality, service and full traceability on par or better. Easy decision, right? What I heard was that it would be too time consuming and that they wanted to stick with their current provider. I later learned that they went back to the distributor who had been ripping them off and the distributor wrote them a check for $1 Million dollars. Now that is true loyalty. Forgive and forget. I have had many experiences just like this over the last 7 years. I can assure you that if a distributor, friend or even family had been taking advantage of me for many years and I knew about it, I would not forgive or forget!!!

I had a client that had 100 locations and was seeing top line revenue decreasing and costs rising. Clearly not what you want to see for your business. My team went in and spent three days in their operations, evaluating where there may be opportunities for savings without sacrificing quality. We found a tremendous amount of opportunity and reviewed this with their team. To achieve this savings, it was going to require multiple product cuttings, labor adjustments because of poor productivity, and many other adjustments that were emotional to the upper management, but would not be noticed by the guest. No surprise, we got the "we really do not have time take this on. We already have too many things in the fire." These were easy fixes and would not only save them money, but would also make a positive impact on their guests and ultimately raise revenue. Unfortunately, these changes never got implemented and the chain went through bankruptcy.

Time is precious, but proper time management leads to a positive impact on your business and life. When you even consider that you do not have time to save money, take a deep breath and then re-consider.

Which tomato do you want? May want to specify.

They type of potato you buy reflects how it will be used.

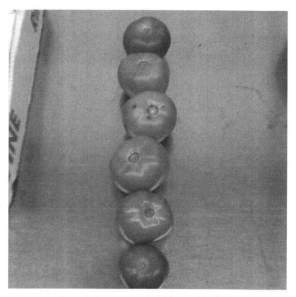

Key Takeaways: No Time to Save Money

"The notion that raising your top line revenue will cure all is not necessarily true. It clearly makes life easier, but it also lulls you to sleep. There are so many ways to save money and many of them are simple and does not require a great deal of time from you or your team. It never costs you anything to listen."

1. **When you wear many hats, you also perform many tasks at a lower level than is required.**

   - Not only are you not the best at everything, in many cases you rush through key decisions simply to get the tasks done.
   - Lack of time becomes an excuse. Yes, some people are afraid that they will be the next cut if they are exposed. The truth is that they should get a raise for bringing in a support system that will save the company money.

2. **Relying on distributors, brokers and manufacturers to make decisions for you may save you time, but not money.**

   - While you do a great job focusing on your top 20 percent of spend, you are potentially grossly over paying for the other 80 percent.
   - Your distributors, brokers and manufacturers are focused on making money for themselves with you a distant second.
   - What you may consider to be an act of friendship may really be something that should be expected of the relationship, or potentially a bribe.

3. **Your business is always in transition.**

   - Too busy is a terrible excuse for taking your eye off your business.
   - Never be too high or too low, and be sure not to become comfortable.
   - Always have a "what if" plan. Be proactive and not reactive.

Be sure to spend lots of time focusing on time management and productivity. This goes for you and your entire team. If you do that, you will never say that you do not have time to save money.

12

TELL PEOPLE WHAT YOU WANT THEM TO BELIEVE: SCRATCH KITCHEN, REALLY?

Over the years, there have been many words used to describe what a restaurant is and how it's different from any competitors. At one time, restaurants were simply about the type of food offered. But now, the industry is so much more crowded that operators must find new ways to stand out from the crowd. When my brother and I opened Fresh City in 1998, we were clearly focused on fresh. Enough so that we put it in our name. We looked at "fresh" as making our food from scratch. We were a regional concept at the time and so we had the ability to produce everything at the location. Yet as the brand started to grow and franchise into new markets, consistency became a crucial focus. We were still using fresh ingredients rather than frozen products, but we started to use certain key manufacturers in our home market to produce our dressings, sauces and soups. The product, became more consistent, and of course, the shelf life dramatically improved. Best of all, the flavor profile did not change and therefore the guests were still happy.

One of the most important things to do as operators is to focus on your story. You must be able to tell the same story in another state that you do in your home city, and I witness this all the time when I consult for emerging chains.

Many of these chains focus on marketing their menu items as scratch cooking, but as they expand outside of their core market, they don't have enough volume to buy local products. Therefore, what was once 'made from scratch' gets pre-prepared or frozen so the term no longer applies and fails to get communicated to the guest. When you build a brand, be sure to make the hard decisions early. Do not live the great lie because your customers will see through those lies. Know what scratch cooking really is and know what your brand can stand behind when market growth starts to occur.

I don't consider buying frozen chicken tenders, dipping them in batter and then frying them up to be scratch, but that is my opinion. I do believe that buying mayonnaise and infusing it with various flavors to create sandwich spreads would be scratch. Gen Z and millennials, overall are focused on the fact that if you say local or scratch, that you are doing exactly that. But, one thing in common with all age groups is that if you are calling out on the menu what is house made, local, organic, fresh, green, environmentally friendly and so on, you will have shown full transparency and will have developed fans of your brand.

Some of the menu descriptions I saw on a Scratch Kitchen menu were: Clam Chowder (Local clams, house made bacon, house croutons), Homemade potato chips (Cut and fried), All dressings that were home-made were identified as such, house cured and smoked wings, local goat cheese, scratch made cookies and pudding, local ice cream, Small family farms (Sustainably raised, free of hormones, antibiotics and steroids). I was very impressed with this menu in that they told me the things that made them different and they did not have to tell me what made them ordinary. I understood that they use local goat cheese and I assumed that their cheddar and provolone were not local. I assumed that it was high quality like the rest of their menu and that was good enough. If they didn't identify that the cookies and pudding were scratch, then I would have assumed that all their desserts were made from scratch, but I am ok that they are not because they were transparent.

One thing I continue to see on menus is "fresh" produce. This may be a bit of overkill in truth in menu. I would be disappointed if my lettuce and tomatoes were frozen. Maybe what some restaurants are saying is that they are cutting their produce in house. I do believe that some produce must be cut in house. Purchasing pre-cut products that have a high moisture content like tomatoes would give you an inferior product, but purchasing fresh broccoli florets vs breaking down cases of broccoli into florets in your kitchen would not be taboo.

The bottom line is that you can say what you want and do what you think, but be aware that there is a very smart consumer out there who may have questions. A few months ago, I was reviewing a supply chain assessment with a client and his tomatoes were incredibly inconsistent. It was driving his staff crazy and his customers were getting very inconsistent quality product and worse than that, my client was paying way too much for this local product. I made my recommendations to the client that quality and consistency should outweigh local when you simply could not get the right product. The client was total against that and countered that they had to be local and could not make a change. So, who really was the beneficiary of this local, overpriced, poor quality tomato?

Frozen chicken battered and fried. Is this scratch cooking?

Key Takeaways: Tell people what you want them to believe: Scratch Kitchen: really?

"You can get away with a lot of things when you describe your brand using a very hot term such as scratch kitchen, but by doing that, you are leaving yourself open to interpretation by a very focused group of customers."

1. **Are you using the term, scratch kitchen for marketing purposes or do you really believe you are a scratch kitchen?**

    - How can a broad menu be totally scratch? Stretching the truth could lead to backlash.

    - What is in your freezer? The bulk of consumers can be somewhat flexible on what scratch is. Frozen foods may have been scratch at one time somewhere, but not in your restaurants.

    - Local is another term which is overused and can really get you in trouble. Most markets do not even have local products available throughout the year.

2. **Is it more important to stay local or scratch at the expense of the food not tasting good?**

    - Be careful not to get caught up in the wrong message. Great food and service remains the priority.

    - Your customers will understand that local may be tough in the middle of the winter.

    - Specify what local means. Provide a distance from your restaurants that you can live with.

3. **Transparency builds tremendous loyalty. Be honest with your customers.**

    - Always better to tell the truth than make it up. I walk into many restaurants who are clearly "misrepresenting the facts" It may say fresh salmon on your menu, for instance, but you may not be able to get fresh salmon, so 86 it!

- Really build up the great things you are doing from scratch. Be proud and talk about it. Quality provides credibility and quantity may say not up to standards.

Be great with what you believe is crucial to what you and your brand are identified with and promote it with pride. You should be good and consistent with everything else and make those things fall under the radar.

13

ONE STOP SHOPPING

In our business and personal life, most of us like to keep it simple. If we could go to one store and buy everything we want, at a price that is reasonable, we would do it. Of course, there are many who like to shop for practical reasons as well as for reasons that make absolutely no sense.

Let's look at some personal examples of one-stop shopping that I believe make my life easier. While I know these retailers are making money off me, they provide me with a convenience and the feeling that I am getting a good deal.

For starters, let's look at Amazon, specifically Amazon Prime. Nothing could be easier than this. I can virtually buy anything I want, get it quickly and with no delivery charge. I also can return the product if it is not right or I don't want it. If I know the product well, especially if it is something I purchased in the past, it is a no brainer for me.

I also love Costco. Being in the foodservice business, I enjoy walking through the food and beverage areas. In typical fashion, I may go there for one or two things and end up with a car load of stuff. Some of these things I simply don't need and other things will last me a year. They may even get me to have a hot dog and drink on my way out of the store. One stop shopping: at a bargain for some things and at a possible premium cost for other things.

Then there is Johnston and Murphy, where I get my shoes. I often go to their outlet location, mainly because I hate the mall, and I find that the outlet has many of the latest styles at excellent prices. I end up buying four pair for the price of three and get a combination of business shoes and casual shoes. At the same time, there may be a deal on socks or belts or clothes. I may have needed one pair of shoes and ended up with my trunk full and some of these shoes are still in boxes in my closet, but I got a great deal, or did I?

Let's shift over to one-stop shopping in the foodservice business. There are clearly some reasons to do this, but many more reasons not to. I have been absolutely shocked at why some of my clients have chosen to do this and how they really did not want to listen to the reality that it was really costing them more money as well as time.

I once had a client with 100+ locations doing very high volume and the supply chain professional I was dealing with insisted on one-stop shopping. One distributor with deliveries of $10,000+ per drop. This is a distributor's dream. Surely, this operator has much more buying power than other smaller brands, but not on everything. Let's review why this operator felt this was in the best interest of his company and then let me tell you what I observed.

Productivity of his team was the first key area. He felt that he could get one delivery three times per week and that was it. There would be less invoices to be paid and he would be an extremely important account of this distributor. All of this, in theory, was very true, but let's look at what was going on. I witnessed deliveries in multiple locations. First, these deliveries were so big that the locations had both of their managers there early in the morning to put these orders away. Not only were they not productive in terms of running production and preparing for the day, they were not thrilled with being the receiving team for deliveries. It also made for a very long day.

Secondly, this truck was delivering everything from fresh proteins to frozen products to fresh produce to dry goods and disposables. This was during the summer and the outside temperature was almost 90 degrees. The temperature in the kitchen felt hotter. I watched the driver turn off his refrigeration (he was cold) and prop open the walk-in cooler door. He was also removing products from the truck and stacking them in the kitchen. The managers were trying to rotate product as quickly as possible, but the driver was quicker than they were. The managers also had to check the invoice. What they were not doing was opening cases and checking for quality as well as looking at dates on the cases.

This chain had put together a fantastic distribution agreement based on the sizes of their drops and the loyalty they had with the distributor, but in reality, their productivity was not as good as it could have been and their pricing on their bottom 50% of spend was only fair because the distributor was dictating what they purchased. Additionally, they were grossly over paying for produce, which should only come from a broad-line distributor when it is necessary. Produce is best delivered on trucks that have only produce so the temperature is correct. It also needs clear specifications from specific growers, which a broad-line distributor typically would not have.

I also had to question this relationship and what was in it for both the operator and the distributor representative. Was it a family or friendship scenario? Were there personal perks involved? What is clear to me is that one-stop shopping in this case was costing this brand money and really needed a non-emotional deep dive into what was in their best interest.

Key Takeaways: One-Stop Shopping

"You may think that one-stop shopping is saving you time and money, but in most cases, it is just the opposite. Usually these decisions are made in an office and not in the operations where the impact is felt."

1. <u>Why choose one-stop shopping in your business?</u>

- Your drop sizes are small and to be able to get a large distributor engaged, you need to increase the delivery size.
- You have locations in highly remote locations and you need your primary distributor to service them. (This is essentially a situation where you potentially picked the wrong markets and the distributor is holding you hostage.)
- That's it!

2. <u>Why you should not use one-stop shopping in your business.</u>

- Affects your productivity negatively and not positively;
- Limits your flexibility on deliver errors or additional needs;
- Puts your distributor into an area of too much influence over you;

- Forces you to purchase items like produce which is not a core competency of a broad-line distributor;
- Lowers the shelf life and ultimately the yield of your products.

3. **Know how a single distributor partner looks at one-stop shopping.**

- Puts them in control of the relationship;
- Gives the operator incredible pricing on the emotional items and socks it to them on the items that they do not pay attention to;
- Sells them as much distributor label product as possible; and
- Provides as many perks as possible to keep the operator loyal.

4. **Your distribution agreement is usually not as good as you think.**

- When you think your agreement is the best in the marketplace and significantly better than other brands your size, rethink what you were thinking! Your distributor is making money in more ways than you know. Regardless of what you may think, they are in business to make money for themselves.

Before you consider one-stop shopping, be sure to evaluate the pluses and minuses of this type of relationship. Beyond the business decision at your office, be sure to get the operations team involved from their perspective.

14

GETTING TO THE FINISH LINE

The key with getting to the finish line starts with a detailed strategic plan. It is always best if we are not in a race to the finish line, but have developed a methodical time-period that has you reaching, although not insurmountable. The other key element about getting to "your" finish line is that you always win if you cross the finish line. Every win will not have a AAA result, but closure of a project, task or sales initiative is paramount.

Let's focus on the strategic plan. It sounds so formal, but it is reality. Even if I was a professional long-distance runner, I would have to put together a strategic plan for how I was going to run and win my next race. I could have emotionally set a goal today to run the Boston marathon a year from now. That is a lofty goal that would require an extremely detailed plan. I am not going to run 26 miles without a strategy. What would my training be? I need to be able to run 1 mile, then 5 miles, then 10 miles, and so on. I need to be prepared for different types of weather. I would also have to be trained for different types of routes. Therefore, I would have to train on hills and valleys. I then need to set goals. Do I want to win the race or was I focused on crossing the finish line to meet or beat a certain time?

The race to the finish line has sure become more complicated! It is now getting close to the race and the weather forecast is showing either rain, high heat or unexpected cold weather. I now must adjust to what I am going to wear and eat or drink. What is my physical condition? Is there anything that will stand in the way of me getting to the finish line? I need to focus on reality and not emotion. I am going to get to the finish line, somehow, someway, but it may not be in the same way that I envisioned a year ago when I came up with my plan.

Now let's look at this from a business perspective. My approach is very simple. First and foremost, I need to come up with a lot of ideas and everyone on my team needs to do the same thing. Some of these ideas are based on a defensive posture and some offensive. Some are short-term focused and some long-term. Most will never get started and some will essentially get to the finish line immediately. This is truly a big win because I didn't have to allocate the time and resources on something that I deemed would end up a loser.

We also must understand that some of the best ideas that generate the most excitement do not become big winners. I remember so many limited time offers and menu items that I put together in my restaurants that I truly believed would be hugely successful. Instead, they were flops. I had a good strategy and a timeline to get to the finish line. There were some signs along the way that were not positive, but tweaks were made and I continued pushing forward. I thought about aborting some of these projects, but I kept rolling because I believed in it and had invested a lot of time and resources in the success of it. What I did learn in many cases was that the products were excellent, but our guests were not ready for them. When my brother and I started Fresh City in 1998, one of our stations was a smoothie and juice bar station. We had studied juice bars in California and were putting it in our Boston brand. Our guests loved the smoothies from day one, but wheatgrass and fresh vegetable juices proved not to be as successful. All of us know how popular juice bars are today. We had the idea, we did the research, the product was great, the execution was excellent, but the result was not there. So, what did we do? We kept innovating. We had a great strategy and we would keep working on what was next.

Let's review some key areas between the idea, and getting to finish line. As reviewed before, we need to come up with a very clear timeline from start to finish. Some projects are short and some are long, but none can be open-ended. There must be an "end game" to every component of a project. What this means is that there must be clear next steps, no matter how elementary the component is. For instance, if you are talking to a potential new catering customer, it is now critical to leave time at the end of your meeting to discuss next steps. Do you need to adjust the proposal? When are you going to talk or meet again? When will the potential client be making their final decision? If you end your meeting hearing, I will be in touch soon, you are usually in trouble.

Be sure to set up an agenda for calls and meetings that allows time at the end for next steps. This agenda is for you and your team, and will keep you on track. You need to remain flexible as the meeting flow is dictated by the client/customer, but under no circumstances can you not leave time for where the project is going, even if the project is over.

Every component of a project essentially has its own mini finish line on the way to the potential big prize. There are wins and losses along the way, but the key is to adjust. We have seen many horse races where the eventual winner comes from behind. There was a plan in place. Your strategy, in most cases, needs to be tweaked along the way, but you can gain momentum quickly and get to the finish line.

You need to keep your focus on the prize.
Coming up short is not an option.

Key Takeaways: Getting to the finish line

"In every case, you must find a way to get to the finish line, even if it involves not winning. An open-ended situation will always result in a drain of time and emotion with very little chance of an ultimate win."

1. **Detailed Strategic Plan: The road starts here**
   - Start with as many ideas as possible, no matter how far-fetched they are.
   - There must be a clear plan to get to the finish line and a key path. This path should include the timing and labor involved.
   - Understand what your ultimate goal is when you get to the finish line. Make sure your expectations are attainable.

2. **Listen and adjust along the way to keep yourself moving.**
   - You can move much faster in a straight line. Peaks and valleys will occur, but you need to adjust to get back on the straight and narrow.
   - All grand plans need to be tweaked constantly. A big project has many smaller projects going on simultaneously.
   - Be careful not to throw darts! You must listen and tweak, but avoid a band-aid approach to changes.

3. **Not every great idea or plan will result in a big win at the finish line.**
   - Do not let things stall. You must avoid anything being open-ended. There should always be next steps on everything.
   - Know when to close a project down when it is not moving forward or you will end up as a loser. Better to get to a finish line quickly as your win will be cost avoidance.

4. **Have an end game to every part of the road to the finish line.**
   - Every element of a strategic plan requires an end game so you can continue the path to the finish line.

- Be sure to have a clear agenda and time line for meetings and calls. Every one of those meetings and calls should have time scheduled to discuss next steps.

It is critical to understand that getting to the finish line is the focus. When you get there, the results will not always be an AAA win, but getting there is a win by itself. Have clear, reachable goals with a strict timeline and don't ever be afraid to end the race early if you feel you will not be able to get to the ultimate finish line.

15

HOW IS YOUR BRAND DIFFERENT?

The first step to answering this question involves understanding your brand from a positioning stand point. Then, you must recognize who your most significant competitors are and who your potential competitors will be. Anyone who is competing with you for customer dollars is a competitor. That includes restaurants, super markets, office cafeterias and cafes, as well as the customer itself eating at home.

Consumers today are driven by very different things than in the past. It used to be very simple, make your food great and your service equally great, and your restaurant will be busy. Let's face it, every restaurant operator thinks their restaurants are the best. They also have some loyal customers, friends and family who tell them how great they area. It is hard to recognize that most of what you do is not the best and if it is the best, someone is working extremely hard to take over the honors.

Who really votes for the majority of the "Best of" yearly surveys? I truly can't believe some of the companies that win for different products. I also see, in many cases, that the same restaurants have won for double digit years in a row. Are they that consistent? Has no one in all these years figured out a way to make a product that is superior? Or, are the winners in the bag?

Winning all the time can sometimes cloud your judgement. It does not push you to stay relevant and focus on being different. When you focus on being the same, even though you are a winner, you will not be prepared for the day when you drop out of first place and your brand has nothing to stand on except for the past.

Back in the 80s, we were making 10 homemade soups per day at Souper Salad. Those soups were mighty good. We of course had our signature daily soups, which we deemed to be the best of the best. Our New England Clam Chowder was one of those items that we were extremely proud of. The goal in developing products was always to make them authentic to the region of origin and then put in a customized twist. Everyone in New England has clam chowder on their menu. Sure, there were restaurants serving it from cans or from frozen batches, but many were making it from scratch. Our focus was to use the freshest of ingredients, including fresh clams, potatoes, and bacon, as well as a fresh clam stock. We used half and half as well to make it a rich and creamy finished product. What made the real difference for us was the number of great products that we put into the chowder. I am sure, like us, you have products that taste good, but have no substance. Many clam chowders have a nice tasty broth, but you can't find the clams. We loaded our chowder with fresh clams and other ingredients. It was a meal and not just a soup. That is what people talked about. To this day, my 93-year-old father-in-law, who loves clam chowder, will go out and have "award winning" chowder at New England restaurants and he will always say, "That was a great chowder, but there are none as good as what you used to make." There was no better compliment than that.

So, how is your brand different? There are so many steakhouses and burger concepts and Mexican fast casuals and sports bars and pizza brands, and on and on. We are also dealing with a consumer base that are not clones. Some want great food, some want great atmosphere. Others want speed and convenience, and still others want no human contact and use technology or social media to interact. Some want to be engaged with you and your brand as a loyal partner and others could care less. Most want great value, but value is viewed very differently from consumer to consumer.

Let's use pizza as an example. Many pizza brands treat their pizza as a commodity and focus on value, order convenience and getting the orders quickly and efficiently through pick-up and delivery. Many of these brands are successful because they do a great job at the basics. They understand who their customers are and will create limited-time-offers centered around additional value such as bundling or buy one, get one. They also will promote pepperoni and other meat pizzas. These concepts are not selling a lot of salads, but they understand who they are. Within this group of commodity pizza brands, they need to understand who their competitors are and find a way to differentiate to gain additional sales. There are also, of course, the Chicago deep dish pizza brands who battle it out in certain markets and they too will tend to claim they are the best, but how are they different. When I visit Chicago, I have my favorite, but it is strictly based on my excellent experiences there. If I was going there for the first time, I would not really know the differences. There is the traditional NY pizza with hand stretched dough. When it is done right, there is none better. Many of these pizzas are cooked to sell as slices. Those big slices really make an impact on the consumer's buying decision.

Then there are the specialty pizza concepts, and there are a lot of them, who are promoting 800 degrees ovens, wood ovens, brick ovens, coal ovens and many other ways of cooking the pizzas. Pizzas are available individually customized and are promoted to be "well done." In many cases, some brands are promoting fresh ricotta, fresh meatballs, wings roasted in the oven and great salads. Many pizzas are very specialized with combinations that you would not expect. Some are casual dining although most are fast casual. Many of these pizzas do not travel well as a crispy, well done pizza because they soften up in the box. If some of these brands can figure that out, they would truly be able to differentiate.

The point I continue to make is that you need to keep your brand relevant. You may have done everything you needed to do when you opened to make your brand stand out as different in a successful way, but don't sit too long admiring your success. There are competitors working on how to match your success and then develop new differentiators to leave you in the dust.

Stand out from others. Don't make the mistake of saying you are better at the same thing. This bourbon distillery made a great impression on me!!

Key Takeaways: How is Your Brand Different?

"If you truly can't answer the question the way a customer would, you need to take a hard look at your business. Maybe your burger is the best in the business because you use a special blend of meats and bake the rolls fresh in house and so much more. But, what if your burger is a nightmare for take-out? Maybe it is so juicy, that when you get home, the roll is soggy and it does not meet the customer's expectations. Maybe you have spent so much time on the burger, but are serving it with a mediocre French fry. What does the guest remember?"

1. <u>**What are you hoping to accomplish with your brand?**</u>
- Who is your clientele and what are their expectations?
- Build loyalty and a buzz. The best way to drive sales is through customers who are raving fans.
- Continue to adjust to your customer's demands. Be a great listener and innovate based upon what you are hearing.

2. <u>**What are the expectations of your customer base?**</u>
- Value - This is universal, but will vary based upon the specific consumer that you are serving.
- Depends on the age group.
- Depends on the locations of your brand.

3. <u>**What is memorable about your restaurant brand?**</u>
- Are you able to quickly list what is truly different?
- Is your list different when you logically think about it?
- Is this the same list that consumers would have?
- Are these differentiators short term and not sustainable?

4. <u>**Don't be lulled to sleep by awards and recognition.**</u>
- Enjoy the accolades, but realize that tomorrow this will be old news. It is easy to be caught up in the hype.

- Being rated the best year after year is something to be proud of, but what happens when you don't get the votes anymore and there is a gap on the plaque hanging in your window?

Being different never stops. The minute you come up with the differentiators and you see success is when you need to start on what will become the next difference maker. You always need to stay one step ahead of the competition.

16

POBLANO PESTO THREE WAYS

Great brands typically have foods with bold flavors. The menu items that customers come back for are memorable and traditionally are assumed to be made from scratch by great talented culinary staff. Unfortunately, most restaurants can't afford those talented people and in general, may not need them to execute great food. Creative thinking is required for a brand to stand out and by developing incredibly creative food you can expand your brand more quickly.

I have worked with many emerging concepts that simply had too many ingredients or products that needed to be stocked at their distributors. A regional chain can easily forget that when they expand to different markets they essentially become an independent in that new market. Sure, they have more buying power in their home market, but it does not work that way when they jump to other distribution centers. The real question is why do these brands have so many items that need to be stocked?

When my brother Larry and I started Fresh City in 1998, we were focused on fresh products made to order at a variety of stations. The ingredients needed to be authentic and have bold flavors. We were dealing with multiple dressings, sauces, soups, sandwich spreads, and so much more. We started out with the fact that our staple, base products had to be the best in quality and flavor. This included our Caesar, Ranch and Balsamic vinaigrette salad dressings, our Teriyaki, Kung Pao and Satay sauces, Chicken Soup, Chili and Clam Chowder, and our guacamole, salsas, barbecue sauce and chicken marinade. There were other items that we were making every day, but we began to use these staple products to develop other products.

From that point on, we began to focus on flavor profiles that would work in any station. There was nothing that said Asian sauces could not be incorporated into sandwich spreads, salad dressings, soups or burrito sauces. Why couldn't we incorporate our Latin flavors from the burrito station into products used at the other stations? Well, we did, and our focus was to use certain key ingredients three times on our menu items. We searched hard for some bold flavors that we did not have the capacity to create and found a company by the name of Sup-herb farms. Among their products were some intense spreads using fresh herbs and peppers. We did a lot of testing and arrived at three products that we would use in three different ways: a poblano pepper paste, a chimichurri paste and a Mexican Chili Lime paste. These pastes were expensive and we needed to get them in from the West Coast to the East Coast. So, to use enough, we needed to be creative. And that is exactly what we did. We were not scientists, but we did call ourselves "chemists." If two or three recipes had outstanding flavor profiles, why couldn't we mix them together to produce bold flavors that no one had ever experienced. Dressings, sauces and soups did not have to be vanilla and could be anything we wanted them to be.

Restaurant brands tend to be pressured into having certain products that the consumer is asking for. At one time it was low fat, then fat free, then gluten free, and on and on. Most of these products that are available in restaurants are terrible. It is simply an obligation. In general, it is like a great steakhouse that sells one chicken item and hopes they never have to serve it. Memorable works both ways. Your guests remember the bad as well as the good. Never discount the person having the chicken, or in my case, the fat free dressing.

So, we went to work on this project in 1998 and never stopped. Yes, we served Poblano pepper pesto three ways. Poblano sour cream was used in our burritos, Poblano mustard was used in our chicken poblano sandwich and our Cactus BBQ sauce was used at our stir fry station. Our Caesar dressing incorporated into mayonnaise to make a garlic and parmesan aioli for a sandwich. The chimichurri paste was used to create an herb goat cheese for sandwiches and an herb marinade for our chicken. Asian sauces were incorporated into our chicken salad, and an Asian slaw was used for a burrito and a pasta salad for catering. Our chicken soup was second to none, but by adding new flavors and ingredients we ended up creating signature soups such as our Asian chicken soup with noodles and our Poblano chicken soup.

I am sure many of you have had great cookies, muffins and other baked goods. Our staples, including chocolate chip and oatmeal raisin cookies, and blueberry and corn muffins, had to be over the top. But, I understood that I could put virtually anything into these cookies and muffins or take some things out. How about a blueberry-corn muffin with fresh corn in it? What about a chocolate chip cookie with dried cherries. We used the same batters and doughs, but incorporated a little imagination.

Your creativity is unlimited. Unfortunately, most brands over think their food and spend way too much on labor, production space, and storage.

It is time to take a clean canvas and think in new ways. Your standards must be over the top, but your entire menu can be bold and keep your business moving forward for a long time to come.

Sup-Herb Farms provided me with incredibly bold flavored pastes that I used for my menu items.

Poblano Chicken Sandwich - Using the paste to develop bold new menu items.

Poblano Chicken
Sandwich

Key Takeaways: Poblano Pesto Three ways

"Bold flavors are all around you and, in many cases, are being under-utilized. Try to work with what you have before you over complicate the culinary aspect of your business.

1. **<u>Customers come back for bold and unique flavors.</u>**
   - They may want a great story, but the food must be great.
   - Listen to your customers. What are they looking for?
   - If they like one item because of a distinct flavor you created, you can then use that ingredient to create another winner!

2. **<u>Chef driven can be very costly to your business.</u>**
   - Beyond your core products, you can develop products by being creative.
   - Some manufacturers focus on extraordinary flavors. Those are the ones you need to work with to enhance your products.
   - Spend every day learning. Listen and read about the next great flavors and see if these flavors are available for you to purchase so you can then develop your next great menu items.

3. **<u>Make sure that your core products are exceptional.</u>**
   - Start with the basics. Without getting too crazy, be sure that basic items are exceptional.
   - Get consumers talking about basic items that, in your restaurants, are not basic at all.
   - Develop great base recipes. For instance, have an incredible chicken soup that requires you to add the chicken, pasta and additional vegetables.

4. **<u>Over thinking your food is costing you in many ways.</u>**
   - Getting things right by producing items from scratch is virtually impossible from location to location.
   - Getting and keeping great people poses a constant obstacle.

- The use of too many ingredients results in overpaying your distributor.

You work so hard at making your brand stand out, but are likely spending your time and money in the wrong places, ultimately losing relevancy. It does not have to be as complex as you are making it. Be creative with the great ingredients and products that you have developed and then use them to take creativity to the next level.

PART THREE

—

BUMPS IN THE ROAD

17

ALWAYS DONE IT THAT WAY

I don't know how many times I have talked to very smart operators about some key opportunities to save money and they pushed back without knowing why. Most of these restaurant executives came on board to lead their respective brands with no emotional ties. I fully understand that it would not be prudent to come in and make wholesale changes without understanding the brand, but I would surely ask a lot of questions. I suppose you could go back to the foundation of the brand and try to understand why they used a specific oil or cheese or paper towel. It is likely that no one is around from that time and even if they were, the reasons why those decisions were made have changed.

Change can be a positive thing to do, if it is done to make your brand stand out. Being innovative and progressive keeps you current. Products are changing, but so is the equipment that you use to prepare the products. The cost of products also has a bearing on what adjustments you make. Keeping the same menu and products constant because that is the way it always has been done can be dangerous to your bottom line.

I did a lot of work for a Mexican fast casual brand that was using exclusively chicken breast. They would not even look at thigh meat, even though most Mexican brands use chicken thighs for their menu items. But this concept was under the assumption that breast meat made them an upscale brand. I can understand that if they were talking about a chicken sandwich or salad with chicken, but in a burrito? Not only that, they were buying jumbo breasts with a high percentage of pump. That was the only way they could get the cost down and it was still significantly more expensive than the thigh meat. The thigh meat also cooked much quicker on the grill, had more flavor and held up better on a steamtable. Well, the chicken breast market went through the roof one year and they decided to test the thigh meat. First it was a 50-50 blend and then all thigh. They never looked back. Their food cost went down, their staff productivity went up and comments from the guests were positive.

The message is that most things should not be sacred. It does not cost you anything to try new products and new ways of preparing the products. Best of all, you can take a couple locations and make them the test locations. Just because you have done it that way forever does not make it right.

At Fresh City, we did a lot of testing. Bold flavors were critical to the brand, but we had to keep our costs in line as we grew. At the time, fast casual was in its infancy and we were only able to get so much money for a menu item. We would never sacrifice quality to get our costs down, so we had to get creative. Like most brands, we used a significant amount of fresh chicken. It started out as all boneless/skinless breasts. It was the least expensive white meat chicken, but it also required the most handling from pounding, to cooking, to cutting. There was a lot of labor involved and a higher risk in terms of food safety. It also was not the right chicken for our burritos. Fresh City was set up with made-to-order stations so our chicken was needed for sandwiches, salads, burritos, and stir fry. Clearly, sandwiches would still be made using chicken breast, but everything else was changed. I developed a process of cooking jumbo tenders together in a half sheet pan. The tenders were marinated in a special herb sauce and then five pounds were placed on a half-sheet pan and roasted. The outcome was one very large piece of roasted chicken, which was cut into cubes and combined with roasted thigh meat. This flavorful chicken was used for stir fry, salads and the burritos. The product was moist, consistent, labor friendly and cost friendly.

One other memorable example was our chocolate chip cookies. It was a exceptional cookie (yes, I am a little biased) with a freshly made dough. As we started to expand to multiple states, we needed a manufacturer to make our dough. The biggest concern was that the cookies would be too uniform. Usually, uniformity is good, but I did not want the product to look like it was being baked somewhere else. We ended up having a 5-ounce puck, which was loaded with chocolate chunks. We cut each puck in half prior to baking and those were used for our bakery. We also cut each puck into quarters prior to baking for catering. The cookies were not perfectly round and the guests loved them. Not everything worked that we tested, but how would we know if we didn't try?

Sure, some things we could not change. This was not because we had always done it that way before; rather, we could not find a better way to do it without sacrificing quality and guest satisfaction. Once you think you have it all figured out, you lose your focus on the big prize. Don't make the mistake of being satisfied with what you have always done. Always strive to make things better.

Is it time to stop fighting to keep a product
that is expensive and unhealthy?

DIETARY FAT	FATTY ACID CONTENT NORMALIZED TO 100%		
MY ORGANIC SUNFLOWER OIL	85%	4%	11%
OLIVE OIL	72%	11%	17%
CANOLA OIL	62%	32%	6%
PEANUT OIL	49%	33%	18%
LARD	47%	12%	41%
BEEF FAT	44%	4%	52%
PALM OIL	39%	10%	51%
BUTTER FAT	34%	2%	64%
CORN OIL	25%	62%	13%
SOYBEAN OIL	24%	61%	15%
LINOLEIC SUNFLOWER	20%	69%	11%
COTTONSEED OIL	18%	55%	27%
SAFFLOWER OIL	13%	77%	10%
	MONOUNSATURATED	POLYUNSATURATED	SATURATED

If it is different, as this is, promote it and challenge others to duplicate

Key Takeaways: Always done it that way

"When you become satisfied with what you have done in the past, you may find yourself getting old and tired very quickly. Surely there are some items that can't be touched, but most items can be reinvented to be better."

1. **Ask questions about everything.**
- Challenge yourself.
- Talk to your customers.
- Talk to your staff.
- Test and then test more.

2. **Times are changing. Very little should be sacred.**
- Manufacturers are watching each other. They will copy popular products and develop better ones.
- Technology allows manufacturers to produce many products that taste better and are more consistent than making them yourself.
- Challenge others.

3. **Your customer is not as loyal to things as you think.**
- Many of your customers' tastes are changing and you need to change with them.
- They have counted on you before for great food, now you must re-invent some things to keep them satisfied.
- Be sure to not just serve things that you like. Let your customers be the judge.

4. **When was the last time you reinvented a product that was good and became great? Can you rattle off three examples quickly?**

- _____

- _____

- _____

Challenge yourself and your team to always get better at what you do. You can lower your food cost, increase your productivity and make your loyal customers come back more frequently.

18

DON'T BS ME!!

Many of us today are so used to being sold to that we do not know what is real and what is fake. We do not know who to trust and, therefore, we tend to put up barriers. I am not sure why we all tend to come back to the used car salesman. Every time I look for a new car, I know exactly what is going to happen at the car dealership. Even if I am totally prepared, know the car I want and have an idea on its price, I will be told that they are running a special deal that day. I will get a price that I know is not even close to their best offer, and that if I have any interest at all, the sales person will go into a secret office and have a talk with the sales manager to see "if they can do better." The sales manager then comes out to see me and just happens to give me a deal that is just over cost. He will do everything to make sure I don't leave the building.

I recently bought a car for my wife and this type of scenario is exactly what I encountered. I told the sales manager that I was going to visit one more dealership before I made the decision. He asked me to call the dealership to get their best price and if it was lower, he would match it. So, I called the other dealership, got somewhat of a lower price, and yes, the sales manager matched it. Was I now below cost? Where did this money come from?

The advantage that a salesperson has when discussing their products to a restaurant or foodservice operator is that they can be prepared. They can, at a minimum, go to the website and look at the menu. They can learn about the company's background, growth, strategies, and so much more. They can then learn about the person they will be meeting with. How long have they been with the company? Where did they work before? And the list continues. They also can find a picture of who they will be meeting with so they walk in with confidence.

Unfortunately, most people selling something are totally unprepared and tend to be a complete waste of time for the potential buyer. I owned and operated Fresh City. Sounds to me like a company that does a lot of things fresh. I had more people coming in to sell me frozen soups, prepared salads and dressings, in addition to many other products. Those meetings lasted five minutes. If someone is not prepared, they do not deserve to have my time or anyone else's within an organization. I made sure that I ended the meeting quickly, but tried to be as helpful as possible so they would not make the same mistake again. Many of these people thank me today because I had an impact on their success. We are not perfect and despite the frustrations we may have, it is important to give back where you can.

Let's flip it around and talk about how restaurant brands BS others. It happens all the time. Much of it is totally unethical and is not something a business professional should be proud of. Unfortunately, you may not be aware of your team's involvement in these situations, but in some cases, you are.

There is clearly a negotiation process going on all the time in your business. Whether it is the purchasing of food, negotiating your distribution agreements, working with designers, contractors, real estate agents, etc. In many cases, you sign an agreement with clear business terms. Think of all the times that you were working with a company or person and you were loyal to them unconditionally. Your contract was expiring and you needed to know if you could do better, so you reached out to others with the sole purpose of using them to lower the cost from your current provider. This happens all the time, but how would you like to be the one on the other end? I assume that you would feel used!

In 2017, I was working with a high-profile restaurant brand in Las Vegas on a produce program that could save them a lot of money. They had been with the same distributor for years and their loyalty was a given. I spent a tremendous amount of time working on their produce program and showed them six figures in savings by using a different distributor. The new distributor had comparable quality products, and service and food safety standards. It also was determined that their 'loyal' current partner had been ripping them off for years. I wish I could say that this brand switched vendors and opted to implement my recommended produce management program. But, they did not. Instead, they confronted their current produce company and received a check for $600k from that vendor. Loyalty can surely be blind!

Let me tell you another story. This one highlights a guest experience that I had at one of my favorite seafood restaurants in Cape Cod. It was the off season and I went to have dinner with my wife there. The restaurant was still busy and the menu was exactly the same as it was during the peak season in the summer. The menu focused in on fresh fish, which was no surprise. My wife ordered the salmon and when she took her first bite it was clearly not very good. I then tasted it and knew right away that this was frozen. I confronted the waiter who had no clue and then the manager came out and informed me that during this time of the year the salmon came in frozen. I asked him why the menu still said fresh. I guess most people did not notice, but this popular restaurant was not being truthful to their guests and they were therefore hurting their business.

Be careful, if it is not fresh, organic, local, grass fed, etc. don't say it is. Highlight and promote the things you are doing, and remember to never BS anyone.

If you are going to charge me for fresh, give me fresh!

Key Takeaways: Don't BS me

"We tend to get extremely agitated when someone is trying to sell us something that we don't need or that has a clear, hidden agenda. But, what if we are doing the same thing to our loyal customers?"

1. **Handling a salesperson who is insulting your intelligence.**
   - Before you meet with someone, be sure that you let them know what the expectations are.
   - Cut off a meeting or sales call quickly if the salesperson is not prepared. End the meeting with a clear statement that will help them in the future. They got the message, no need to berate.
   - Ask the salesperson to cut to the chase. You want to see the decision maker sooner than later. Or, if you are presented with a presentation that has pages and pages of BS, ask to move on to the pricing.

2. **Are you prepared to meet with a client or customer?**
   - You and your team should know everyone attending a meeting.
   - Prior to the meeting, there should be clear expectations so you can formulate an agenda. Ask basic questions prior to the face-to-face meeting.
   - Be aware of their time. Be very visual and not too wordy.

3. **Being used and using others.**
   - Pick your spots as your reputation can be affected quickly.
   - Go to the incumbent first and not last. Ask them for their best pricing and let them know that you are going to their competitors. They must believe that they can lose the business.
   - Always remember when you were used so you can understand it from the other side.

4. **Truth in menu: sometimes.**
   - Once you are exposed, you will never recover.
   - Promote what you can and be sure it is consistent long term.

- Talk to your staff. It is better to 86 an item rather than serve something that is inferior.

Be sure to focus on the things you do great or on the items that you consistently talk about. Once you begin to be a story teller instead of an honest business person, you will ultimately lose your credibility.

19

BUILDING THE RIGHT TEAM: LABOR PRODUCTIVITY

Labor has become a major roadblock to financial success in the food-service industry. The cost of labor has skyrocketed and the pool of talented people who want to work in the industry has decreased. We have all seen incredibly talented people within our organizations as well as enthusiastic, hard-working people who service us every day in restaurants, retail, and so many other areas of our daily life. The question is how do you judge the value of an employee?

In the foodservice business, labor is typically the second highest expense item after food. I look at labor in terms of how it will affect my top line revenue and how it could have an impact on my food cost. The people in your organization create the culture that will drive customers back. You have the ability to hire the right people who can have a tremendous impact on your business.

For the most part, I had the opportunity to lead a business and develop a great culture. I focused on hiring people who worked hard, wanted to be part of a team and wanted to grow both personally and pro-fessionally. I communicated regularly with my whole team, discussing how they were doing, how they could improve and how the organization could improve. This included my executive team as well as my dishwashers. They all had an important role within the organization. Some clearly had more responsibility and got paid more, but my expectations of them were higher. I was not a leader who sat at a desk and demanded results without under-standing what was going on in the restaurants. Yes, I very much demanded results; however, my team was on the same page regarding expectations.

For more than 30 years of operating multiple companies, I spent almost every day at the restaurants during lunch. I also spent time there during breakfast, dinner and at prep. I am extremely structured and put top notch systems in place for my company, but how do you write training manuals and systems without understanding what is going on at the store level. When developing menu items, the product had to be excellent and the execution had to be flawless. So, we brought in team members that had some inherent hospitality skills and decided to teach any additional skills when necessary. I spent many days working side by side with hourly prep staff, line staff and others because I wanted to understand what they did and how it could improve. I wanted to understand things from the guest point of view on wait time, customized food options and anything else that I could learn. To this day, I have former team members who thank me for teaching them and having an impact on their lives. I simply cared about them and wanted them to excel. When our employees are thriving, our businesses succeed as a result.

If all you are looking for is the cheapest labor, you will get poor productivity and it will cost you money. Some important things to consider is that experience, age, and longevity at a company do not constitute a positive or negative impact on what type of employee you will end up with. It clearly depends upon the individual. I have personally worked for two companies throughout my career and ran my own business for the rest of the time. One of the companies I worked for took a young guy out of college, who had a lot of spunk and the desire to learn, and turned him into a professional hospitality operator. I learned so much from so many people and I worked as hard as a person could work. I loved the business and wanted to keep learning and moving forward with my career. Whatever they were paying me was not enough, but the education I was getting was well worth it. Note that there were other managers, likely making much more money than me, who were there for a job with no desire to grow. Seeing how those managers performed shaped my view on compensation. People should be paid based on more than how long they have worked for you. In fact, if a person has worked for you for many years in the same position, they are likely not providing the value that you think.

My second instance of working for someone else came after I sold my restaurants. I had a lot of experience and a tremendous desire to be successful. I was given an opportunity to use my skills to support an organization early on in their growth cycle. It was great opportunity and one that I continue to appreciate. There were certain skills that I needed to learn so I could be successful in my new position and I was taught those skills. I also was paid well to perform in a major position for my employer. I built a great organization during my time there by putting together a great team. I brought in talent who knew how to execute and they were worth every penny. I felt the same about myself. People are not clones and should be judged on their own merits. You clearly get what you pay for.

How you produce is how you should be judged. This also is a factor with age. The question I always answer when interviewing people is whether the person is on the way up or on the way down. People on the way up are focused on using their experience to make a difference and they also want to learn every day. They want to grow and to have a purpose. I once sat on an airplane with a gentleman who was 87 years old. He was in the real estate development business and was incredibly focused. I asked why he was still working at 87. He answered that he loved what he did and enjoyed the opportunity to learn from others so he could continue to get better. I loved this guy. He was speaking my language. A company should be balanced with different age groups and different core competencies, but experience should never be looked on as a negative just because that person may need to get paid more. If you pay more, no matter what their age, you should have higher expectations of that individual.

One other important thought on labor productivity is if you hire someone and they are not meeting your expectations, you need to confront the situation head on. Most people want to do well and some simply have no desire. They may have been hired based on need and had a good initial interview, but how they execute is what you need to look at. I am a big believer in great communication. I like to ask the team member how they feel they are doing and how they can improve. If a person is not going to meet your expectations, they should be the ones who make the decision.

Regular communication gets that done. If not, a mutual decision to part ways may be best for all involved.

Does the person you hired to purchase food know what they are doing?

Great products require quality labor.

Key Takeaways: Building the right team: Labor Productivity

"Your culture will breed great people and those people will help grow your organization and make it profitable. Hiring the least expensive employees, who meet certain requirements on paper, is comparable to throwing darts. You may get lucky, but in most cases, you will waste time and money."

1. **Does your culture breed talent or potential incompetence?**
   - A new hire must fit in to the culture that you have created.
   - It is about the team and not just the individual.
   - A good hire must be nimble and adjust to the needs of the organization.

2. **How detailed are your job descriptions?**
   - What are you looking for and is the applicant the right fit?
   - Can the person you hired exceed expectations within a year and then move on to another role?
   - Be sure that the expectations of the position are clear from day one.

3. **Knowing how and when to cut off a staff relationship**
   - Set expectations early and often.
   - Stick to a 30-day evaluation and do another one 90 days later.
   - Ask questions of the team member and let them conclude that they may not be a good fit.

4. **How do you measure productivity?**
   - Speed of service;
   - Yield and lack of waste in the kitchen;
   - Time management; and
   - Organizational skills.

It is understood that you have a budgeted amount for labor, but you may pass on some incredible talent if sticking to your budget is your only focus. Be sure to keep your eyes on talent, especially if they have a big upside.

20

ARE YOU USING THE RIGHT PRODUCT FOR THE JOB?

There are so many factors that determine whether you are using the right product for a specific job. Unfortunately, many of these factors are not looked at by professionals in the hospitality industry. Some of the reasons are lack of time, lack of desire to make changes, lack of industry knowledge on available products, job security issues, lack of infrastructure to roll out a change, and emotional issues that result in being close minded. We will touch on each of these and review how embracing this can make a major difference in your business.

The hospitality industry has so many options for new products, new packaging and new ways of doing things. Technology has provided the ability to have quality, consistent products with extended shelf life. In some cases, we try to force our restaurants to do scratch cooking and heavy culinary-based production. Unfortunately, the team members involved do not have the skill set to produce the high quality, consistent products that you have specified at your corporate office. You, therefore, are marketing great things to your guests, but your execution is far below the standards.

Every situation is different and requires creative thinking by the leadership team to get it right. What you want is not always necessarily what you get, so you need to be open to making bold decisions. If you are a regional chain, you can control things much better than if you are national one. However, once you have locations in multiple states, you are susceptible to inconsistent products and that is where your brand can begin to downward spiral. When Fresh City opened their first location in 1998, we had a commissary and were producing numerous products. As we expanded into multiple states, we had to eliminate the commissary and get some of our key products made by top-notch manufacturers. I also had to make sure that our franchisees had access to the required products needed to run their restaurants in a way that was reflective of our corporate locations. We did not have the space, culinary expertise or desire to produce many of our products at the store level, but their quality and consistency could not skip a beat.

A signature product like our clam chowder was put in the hands of a manufacturer who was able to duplicate the original recipe, keep it refrigerated and provide a 21-day shelf life. Yes, the product cost was more per ounce than producing it in house, but was it really?

It is a given that you do not want to lower your quality or raise your food cost. However, sometimes you need to pay more to pay less. You may ask how is that possible? As restaurant operators, there is a tendency to look at the least expensive option on most things without factoring in labor, waste, yield, and storage. For example, let's take broccoli. You purchase broccoli in three common ways: 14-count with full stem, broccoli crowns or and florets. Without question, the 14-count with a full stem is the least expensive, but is it really? Are you using 100% of the broccoli, including the stem? How much time does it take to prep the broccoli and what kind of yield are you getting? If all you are looking for is broccoli florets, your least expensive option is to purchase just the florets.

Have you considered the package size of what you buy? Many of you have a mark-up from your distributors of a fixed-fee per case. They would like for you to buy the smallest case possible, yet you should want to buy the largest case possible, if you can use the product before it expires. You also may be buying product in retail packaging. If that is the case, you are actually paying for that and it is slowing down your staff, adding more trash and lowering the product's shelf life. Lettuce and tomatoes are the two biggest produce examples of this and they tend to be the highest-volume produce items that you purchase. Retail grape tomatoes come in an 8.5-pound case and are packaged in 12 individual plastic containers. Bulk grape tomatoes come loose in a 10-pound case. The bulk product is easier to handle, creates less trash, and can save operators up to 20%. The same is true for romaine hearts. Each bag at the grocery store typically holds three hearts and they are packed 12 per case. You could save 15% if you purchased 48-count bulk romaine hearts, and cut back on labor and trash while improving your yield.

Disposables also are a major source of purchasing dollars and operators tend to not pay enough attention to these items. Paper towels are a great example. I see large companies using C-fold towels and, as I grab 20 towels, I see many more lying on the floor. Restaurant operators could save 30% if they went with a hands-free, rolled paper towel, and they would make their customers much happier. The same holds true with dispenser napkins. Using proper dispensers that allow your customer to take one at a time instead of a large stack that they will never use adds up to big savings.

Proteins are the most sacred items of all and they, in many cases, are where the most money is being wasted. Any product that requires trimming and needs to be weighed should be a red flag. Trimming the perfect amount of fat off a piece of meat requires a person who is excellent with a knife and even that person under the pressure of speed can have mixed results. This means there will be times when even usable meat ends up in the trash. Then, there is the weighing of the product, which requires an accurate scale. So, if the scale is off, so too is its weight. In many cases, a quality protein that is individually packaged to your spec weight will save you money despite it costing you more per pound.

Continue to question whether you are using the right product for the job. You will be glad you did because it could save you money in labor and food cost, eliminate some food safety issues, potentially decrease your kitchen footprint, and ultimately make you more consistent.

Which way should you purchase broccoli? Are you using the stems?

14 Count Broccoli   Cut Crowns Broccoli   Pre-cut Florets Broccoli

Which pack size is best for you? Bulk will save you 20%.

Are you using a retail pack? You can save 15%.

Key Takeaways: Are you using the right product for the job?

"The hardest part of knowing whether you are using the right product for the job is to be able to ask the right questions. A great organization has to always challenge themselves as things change, and you need to change with it."

1. **Lack of time and resources**
- If you do not have time to evaluate your business then you need to re-evaluate how you spend your time.
- There are many people within an organization who can be involved in product evaluation. Once you set the parameters of what needs to be done, you can motivate key team members to get engaged.
- Not having the resources to roll out something is simply an excuse. When something is right for your customer and your business, you need to see things through.

2. **Lack of desire to make changes**
- Don't be fooled by bumps in sales and profits. Your costs can take a spike very quickly. Don't wait for it to happen.
- Always done it that way is an incredibly lazy approach to life.
- Complacency in the restaurant business will lead to reduced sales and profits.

3. **Thinking you are protecting your job by hiding opportunities**
- When things are done the same way for a long period of time, begin to question what the motive is of others.
- Too many decision makers have a personal agenda vs a company agenda. Status quo is easy, challenging yourself can be hard, but will ultimately lead to great rewards.
- Be sure that there is a monthly innovation discussion in your organization for all key people. Everyone must be prepared to discuss new and different ways to help drive revenue, reduce costs and improve productivity.

4. <u>**Being misled by your "so called" partners**</u>

- Never forget that your partners are focused on themselves first and you second. Challenge them. Don't assume your interests are first on their list.

- Don't just spend time having lunch at your restaurants. Dig deep and get into your kitchen and storage. You will see things that you will question.

- Be aware of what is new in the industry. Stay sharp!

A quality operator and person will always question what they are doing. There are many ways to get to a positive outcome, but in most cases, making well thought out adjustments can reduce your costs, increase your productivity, decrease your kitchen footprint, and provide added consistency

21

PAY BY PERFORMANCE

Wouldn't it be great if you could watch a movie, a sporting event, a play or go to a restaurant and experience it before paying? If you liked the performance you would pay more than if you didn't. This, of course, is never going to happen, but one thing would be guaranteed, most of the performances would be at a higher level than they are today. It is no surprise that a professional athlete in the last year of his contract, "the contract year," will perform at a higher level. It also is very common that when an athlete signs a long-term contract, they get complacent and do not perform to the level that they are paid.

Many people simply perform because they love what they do and feel that they have a responsibility to do it right. I believe that if you need to do something, you should give everything you have to do it at a high level. Usually, it takes the same amount of time to do something well vs poorly. My feeling is that anyone who performs at a consistently high level, should be acknowledged and compensated accordingly.

That is why it is very important to get to know your employees. Sometimes the smallest things make the biggest difference. What do they enjoy doing outside of work? Maybe sports or travel or any number of things. A salaried employee is usually given a raise once per year. If they perform well during the year, they should be taken care of. I am a big believer in the intangibles. I have always expected quality performance from my teams and it was my responsibility to communicate what the objective was. If an employee was going above and beyond, I made sure that I got them tickets to something they enjoyed or sent them to a restaurant for dinner. It is so important to recognize performance and never take it for granted. Great employees can work for anyone and be successful. Loyalty has tremendous value.

What about a tipped employee? They should have to perform at a high level to get a great tip. I can't stand getting a check where the tip is included. Why am I paying a service fee when I haven't gotten any service yet? You see this in many restaurants, catering events and room service. When service is included, in many cases, the service level is sub-par. This basically falls into pay for no performance or possible performance. A tipped server can get significant gratuities if they perform at a high level. Are you someone who is a bad tipper? Why would a customer give less than 15%? That is really the bare minimum if a server performs at a standard level. It happens all the time and it is totally unacceptable.

It also is important, whenever possible, to know some of the things your customers like. What is interesting is that our catering customers may be performing for us without us really knowing it. They are hosting catering events and bringing in potential new catering customers. They surely want everything to be perfect at their event. We are performing for them and they are performing for us. A frequent catering customer should get certain perks. At Fresh City, we used to provide something to our key catering customers six times per year. It was cupcakes and chocolates and other things which were not costly, but had a lasting impact. We were providing a little additional benefit for loyal catering customers who were indirectly working to build our business.

Another version of pay by performance involves how we treat those customers who come to our restaurants frequently. Some restaurant brands do loyalty cards and that is a perk that you provide based on performance. There is a balance that must take place between the customer and the operator, but clearly it is the operator who must be the true performer. A customer will come back for many reasons, but ultimately, it is great food and consistent service that will bring them back.

I also have had the opportunity to see how pay by performance can involve some unethical and nasty outcomes. I was brought up to be very honorable and when I made a deal, I stuck to the deal. During the negotiation part, you can be as tough as you want to be, but when the deal is done, you should stick to it. As a consultant to restaurant brands, most of the people I dealt with could not have been more professional and would never have tried to do what is wrong, but some of the so called bad apples really stood out.

In one instance, I had a 50-unit chain that signed on for a one-year agreement for my team to support them with cost reduction, product sourcing and in general an overall partnership to help them as they were growing. My team found a bunch of easy savings and then started to crack some larger savings on some high-volume items. The contract stated that we would get 20% of the savings. This was the same contract that we had in place for everyone else and is deemed to be very fair. After saving this chain six figures, they did not want to pay us our 20%. They claimed it was too much. It was OK when the contract was signed, but not OK after we saved them the money. How would this company like it if they served a great meal to a customer and then when the bill came, the customer decided that they were not going to pay. They reasoned that they did not see the same value from the price that was on the menu. I bet that the CEO running this company would have flipped out. You can't have it both ways.

If you are clear on what the parameters are on a pay-by-performance relationship, then you or your customer should adhere to the agreement. There should be no grey area. In most cases, it will be a win-win situation.

A sense of entitlement is the worst thing you create for your company: I have always made sure to visit the source before recommending to my clients.

There should be clear expectations on both sides to judge performance

Key Takeaways: Pay by Performance

"Performance should be the key element to what you get paid and how you are looked at in the long term. Entitlement based upon friendship, family and past performance is very dangerous as it results, in most cases, in mediocre performance."

1. **Performing as if it is the last year of your contract**
   - Focus on always trying to learn and get better.
   - Look at different ways to improve your performance.
   - Never become complacent. The timing of your contract should not impact the quality of your performance.

2. **Set clear expectations for you and the people you are working with**
   - When you agree on something that will be performance based, the expectations must constantly be measured.
   - Every time you meet someone's expectations, you must then set new expectations moving forward.
   - Inconsistency creates a feeling of disappointment. If you can't execute on a consistent basis, you will fall short on performance.

3. **Take care of the loyal people who appreciate your performance**
   - Never take these loyal people for granted as they can leave you very quickly.
   - Understand how you can provide something to these loyal people that they do not expect.
   - Be sure to avoid stepping over the line from business to personal when possible. The relationship will become cloudy if you do.

4. **Honor your agreements the same way that you would expect others to honor the same agreement**
   - Be careful not to get so full of yourself that you are beyond fulfilling your part of an agreement.

- Treat people with respect. If you don't, some of these people you disrespected will end up in a position where they can get you back.
- When a customer takes advantage of you without cause, think about how you may have done this to others.

Pay by performance is an ongoing process that results in long term success if you continue to push forward. Complacency leads to mediocre performance and ultimately failure. You should never think that you have it all figured out.

22

BREAD AND COFFEE

How many times have you gone to a restaurant and had a great meal with great service, but were incredibly disappointed by the either the bread basket and/or the coffee? It is so common for restaurant brands to use some great ingredients and then combine them with some other inferior ingredients. The effort that you have put into giving your guest a great experience will go for naught as they will remember the mediocre components.

Like many people, I love great bread. I know it is not good for me and I am eating too many carbs, but great bread on a sandwich, with a salad, with a burger or at the beginning of a first-class dinner, makes a lasting impact on my experience. Bread should not be an after-thought. It also should not be purchased strictly based on cost. Don't you love that artesian crusty bread served with olive oil or pesto or homemade spreads. Bread can make a meal memorable. One of my favorite restaurants is called Sweet Basil. It is a chef-driven neighborhood restaurant with an Italian/ Mediterranean menu. The food, atmosphere and service are incredible, but everyone talks about the delicious focaccia bread served with fresh basil pesto. I know it may cost the restaurant owner more to give this bread and pesto away (the cost is really part of the overall cost of the meal), but it is one of the reasons this restaurant has a wait every day of the week.

This chapter is not really about bread and coffee, even though I will bring up coffee later. This is about having consistent standards. The consumer today is very educated on what they are eating and drinking. We have all experienced food and service issues during certain days or times in restaurants. As a consumer, you always wonder why the service is so poor when the restaurant is the slowest. You also see incredible inconsistency on a Sunday or Monday, when compared to the great food you had on Friday or Saturday.

At Fresh City, I went through this every Sunday for a short while. It was a learning experience for me. You can never accept anything that falls below the standards of the brand. My customers did not pay me for less than the best so why was I serving less than the best? One of our signature items was the salad wrap. Customers loved salad wraps and wanted them for lunch and dinner seven days a week. We received fresh pita bread in our restaurants every morning. Unfortunately, in the early days of Fresh City, we did not get deliveries on Sunday. We did everything we could to make that pita bread great on Sunday, but it would never be as good as the other six days. Within 30 days, we found a way to get our pita baker to deliver on Sundays, but how many customers did we let down before then?

There are so many examples of where a restaurant brand goes all out to make a meal fantastic, but they miss a key element that would make the items memorable. Burgers come to mind as an example of this. The basic ingredients of a standard burger involve the roll, burger, cheese, lettuce, tomato, and onion. It clearly starts with the burger, so if the quality of your meat is sub-par, nothing else matters. We also have seen rolls that are too big, too small, not fresh, too soft, and too hard. The most important thing about the roll is that it complements the burger. Now, on to the cheese. If you use cheddar, use a sharp, quality cheddar. Do not save money by using an American cheese type of cheddar. Finally, there is the lettuce, tomato and onion. Many places simply take this for granted. Be sure to specify an onion that does not overwhelm the burger. Your customer purchased a burger and not an onion. The lettuce needs to have proper coverage and be the right texture.

Lastly, there is the tomato. Tomatoes are what drive me crazy. I have seen so many brands do a great job on their burgers and then ruin them with a under ripe, tasteless tomato. Use one large tomato slice that is neither too firm or too ripe. If a tomato is too firm, it has no flavor, and if one is too ripe, it leaves a mess. Additionally, do you really want three tomato slices on a burger that are falling out? Like everything else, what you do requires a lot of thought.

I have been saving coffee to talk about last. Customers are addicted to their coffee in the morning, and serving coffee is so much more complicated today than in the past. Most companies offer a light, medium and dark roast, but the differences between these roasts vary significantly from place to place. Another difference is how brands serve their coffee to guests. Some put the milk and sugar in for you, while others give customers black coffee with the opportunity for them to customize their coffee on their own. It doesn't really matter who does what, as long as the coffee is consistent and good, and employees are properly trained to make a great product.

For 10 years I went to my local Peet's Coffee because Bob, my barista, made my latte exactly the way I wanted it. It looked like the picture in the window, tasted great, and I looked forward to it every time I went there. One day, Bob told me that he was leaving Peet's to become a real estate broker. I was sorry to see him leave, but I figured that whomever replaced him would be well trained. I was wrong! I continued to be disappointed and I finally stopped having lattes. They no longer looked like the picture and didn't taste up to standard.

Of course, there are now so many coffee options which made it easy for me to find my new perfect latte. However, I continue to drink my Peet's Major Dickinson for drip coffee. My experience begs the question: How often do consumers have a food and beverage experience where the product does not match the picture or the description?

Everything we do now is under a microscope. Be sure to carry your mission straight through everything you do. Your customers will appreciate it and they will come back often.

On top is a picture of my latte I am drinking right now!

Below is something called a latte, but what a disappointment!

Key Takeaways: Bread and Coffee

"Most brands fail to carry through the quality and consistency of their products from beginning to end. Failing to match the standards of even one ingredient could ruin he quality of your menu item and drive you customers away."

1. **What is going into your bread basket?**
   - Make it memorable, even if you need to charge for it.
   - Develop spreads or oils to go along with bread.
   - Alter the textures, to widen its appeal.

2. **Do you take certain ingredients for granted?**
   - Never treat a commodity, such as a tomato, as a commodity.
   - Make sure that all potential menu items go through vigorous testing before they become permanent.
   - Be sure that ingredients used in menu items are available year-round at the same consistency that you tested them.

3. **The quality of your menu items should be the same whenever your guests have them**
   - Test your menu items at all times of the day and week.
   - Have a clear understanding of the shelf life of your ingredients.
   - Think like a customer and you will have greater success.

4. **How does coffee play out in your world?**
   - Are you drinking a coffee that is different than what your guests are looking for?
   - Do you treat the quality of your coffee the same as your food?
   - Do you buy your coffee strictly based on raw cost per pound?
   - When you go out for a meal and the bread and coffee are ordinary, and in some cases, memorable in a bad way, think about your own concepts and whether what you are doing needs to be adjusted. Never assume that everything is perfect because your guests are constantly judging you.

23

SETTING EXPECTATIONS: DON'T GET FOOLED BY THE LINES.

We have all been there, whether as an operator or as a customer. It is opening night and there are lines of people waiting to eat at the next big restaurant. There have already been pre-openings and word on the street is that this is the place to go.

There is an army of employees working and a lot of "executives," who are watching and learning and, most of all, kissing babies. Nothing is going to go wrong while the corporate training team and corporate executives are in the building. The reviews will be great, the word will be out and business will be booming. However, little by little the corporate team leaves and it is now up to the local team to sustain the opening buzz. The question is what expectations have now been set for this restaurant and can they meet those expectations? It is unlikely that a staff of new people can execute in the same fashion as the seasoned corporate team. That is, unless the foundation is properly set.

There must be very clear expectations of how your brand will operate from the beginning. What should the typical wait time be? How long should it take to get your food and beverage? How often should the restrooms be checked? How many times should a guest be communicated with from a team member? There are hundreds of these questions that should be answered by you and the corporate team, and then reviewed with the new team during the restaurant opening. Why should it take five minutes to get your food at the opening and then 10 minutes once the corporate team leaves? You must set the expectations of your guest early and often. If there is clarity for both the restaurant team and the guest, it will be easy for both to meet expectations.

Based on your experience, you should be able to develop a timeline that focuses on how long it takes for a server to go from four to five to six tables. Or, how long it will take before a cashier can handle the rush during peak times. In terms of fast casual, how many sandwiches or burgers or pizzas or salads can a team member make within a given time? One of the mistakes commonly made is that we develop a budget based on what the labor schedule should be as opposed to what labor is needed while the staff gets their necessary experience. I hope that whoever developed this schedule, and the standards associated with its execution, spent time in the operations field as opposed to behind a desk.

Anyone who has been involved in the hospitality industry has dealt with setting expectations. How about pre-meal meetings where the team gets together to discuss reservations, specials and anything else pertinent to the shift ahead. What about the kitchen manager or other restaurant leaders who do line checks for every shift so they can taste the food and eyeball the freshness. There are clear expectations here. Have you ever "not had time" to check your line? I call that, no time to catch a potential disaster. You are playing poker if you do not know what to expect.

Let's look at a professional basketball or football team. They are not that much different than that of a restaurant team. The coach/manager has set clear expectations regarding the type of individuals they are looking for to make a great team. Some of the people will be experienced and some will have potential. Some will have roles specific to a position, while others will be hybrids or utility team members. Regardless, there should be clear job descriptions for all positions. They should know what the expectations are and you should judge them accordingly. Of course, you also must set clear expectations for the trainer. The trainers have the task of getting these individuals up to speed and part of the team culture. Imagine a basketball team that did not evaluate their next opponent and just kept playing the same game. This simply does not happen. The coach reviews tape, understands the opponent and reviews team expectations as well as individual ones.

After nearly seven years of consulting, I had 200 clients of different sizes, with very different objectives. There were emerging chains, mature brands, multi-concept restaurant companies, casinos, hotels, theme parks, and corporate feeders. Not one of them was the same. They varied from quick service, fast casual, casual dining to fine dining. One thing they did have in common was that they all had a clear vision of what my team and I were expected to accomplish. My job was to make sure there were clear expectations both from the client and my organization. A partnership can never be one-sided and therefore the parameters of the partnership had to be set. There needed to be established long-term expectations and then there needed to be short term ones that we used to benchmark our progress.

If you are successful with a client-consultant partnership, just like the long line at the restaurant, you do not stop providing additional support. Your client's expectations would be to ask you what is next. Unfortunately, you do not have the luxury of dwelling on your past successes. Complacency can lead to a termination notice.

Great organizations have great leaders. They tend to be good communicators and set clear expectations for themselves and their teams, with both short-term and long-term goals. Throwing darts at things may work at times, but in the long run, they will begin to miss the target. When you see that long line or you look at a month of revenue and profits that far exceeded your expectations, smile, give you and your team a pat on the back and then dig deep to work on what's next. You do not want to be the one who looks at dwindling sales and ask what happened.

Key Takeaways: Setting Expectations: Don't get fooled by the lines

"Everyone, to some degree, are setting expectations both personally and professionally. Staying on top of these expectations and adjusting them as needed will help you avoid disappointment and create rewarding outcomes."

1. **Keeping the long line at opening a long-term vision**

- Look at the long line, smile and figure out how to keep customers coming into the door.
- Be sure to understand whether you are at capacity or moving too slow to service the people in line.
- Do you see people leaving at the back of the line?

2. **Determining realistic expectations of how your restaurants should run**

- Create detailed job descriptions that are clear to both you and the team member.
- What can team members realistically do from day one to specific time periods?
- Develop hybrids or utility people who can be multi-taskers.

3. **Communication with your team**

- Are you on the same page with your team regarding expectations?
- Has your team engaged with you as to where things are and how they can continue to improve?
- Challenge your team. Innovation is the key to an ongoing relationship. Raise the bar on your expectations.

4. **Expectations must be understood by both sides of the partnership**

- Someone is going to be disappointed if both sides do not agree on the expectations.
- Communicate where you stand with expectations on a regular basis and adjust accordingly.

- Old news, even if it is good news, is not enough to keep a relationship strong. What have you done for me lately?

Always reach high and adjust if your expectations are going to be difficult to meet. At the same time, if you are meeting your expectations early in the process, raise the bar and shoot for the stars.

24

HOSPITALITY: BEYOND THE FOOD

Quality food is a given. Without providing your guests with the quality food that they expect, you will be out of business. It is no surprise that the bulk of time spent on a brand revolves around the food. Clearly you have to stand out from the crowd with your food and continue to differentiate from your current and future competitors. We now need to discuss the many intangibles which can take you to the next level. For the most part, the food is not enough to keep customers coming back. They are looking for other things that will make them loyal.

Hospitality has always been associated with hotels and fine dining restaurants. Hospitality is defined as "the friendly and generous reception and entertainment of guests, visitors or strangers." When you visit a hotel, you expect hospitality even before you arrive to check in. There needs to be a simple process of booking your room and getting the confirmation that shows how great your stay will be when you arrive. When you arrive at the hotel, the door man should greet you, help you with your luggage and possibly park your car. When this is executed well, you should immediately feel that they are happy to have you as their guest.

It is now time to check-in. You can check-in remotely, but most guests prefer to talk to someone behind the front desk. They are typically extremely helpful and welcoming. They tell you where to find things in the hotel, answer your questions and send you to the elevators to get to your room. There is a concierge available to help you with your reservations to restaurants and activities, and everyone in the hotel is saying hello to you to make your stay is a great one. If you need anything, you just call and it will be there. Everyone is trying to accommodate you. This is the way hospitality should be.

My wife and I recently went to a high-end restaurant to celebrate her birthday. I made my reservation through Open Table and I provided them with a note acknowledging that it was her birthday. We arrived at the restaurant and valet parked. I was immediately told that I would be receiving a text and that I could request my car and pay from that text. We went in and were greeted, and then seated at our table. My expectations were that the food would be excellent. At $50 per entrée, I would hope the kitchen would know what they were doing. I liked the waiter immediately. He was knowledgeable, professional and welcoming. When we asked about certain entrees, he did not recommend the most expensive items. He was extremely honest and made you feel like a true guest. We shared a salad and they split the salad in the kitchen. That is the way to serve properly. The entrees came and my steak was cooked perfectly. The server even waited for me to cut into my steak to make sure I was happy. Our plates were cleared at the same time, as they should be, and the tablecloth was cleared of crumbs. The waiter tastefully brought over a dessert for my wife's birthday, which we shared. There was no point that we did not feel taken care of and when the manager checked in with us at the end of the meal, we knew that they were on top of their game. The level of hospitality at the restaurant will make us come back. The food was great, but the intangibles will bring us back.

We have all encountered experiences where service was slow and the food was not up to your standards. It is not feasible to be perfect every time, but it is how you handle negative situations that can potentially differentiate you. A less than stellar experience requires solutions that brings the customer back. You must satisfy the customer's needs for their current meal, but also something to get them back for another chance. Free meals alone will not solve the problem. It is the level of hospitality that brings you back. I once went to a popular steakhouse and the overall experience was not great. Our table for six was very close to a larger party that was extremely loud. We had to yell to hear each other. Couple with that, the food was not up to standards. The manager came over and did everything right which ended with serving dessert. One dessert was outstanding and I told the manager. After comping the meal, he came over to me with a whole cake for me to take home. He exceeded expectations and the problems earlier became old news and I looked forward to trying the restaurant again.

The key to great hospitality is understanding who the guest is and what they want as an experience. The first thing you should do is pick out who the host is at the table. They are typically the one who will be paying and dictating the level of service. Is this going to be a business meeting, a celebration, a first date, a wedding proposal, or lunch after a funeral? Every situation requires a certain level of hospitality. You need to get a sense of what that level is. You may simply have a loyal customer who just needs to be acknowledged with a hello and thank you. And, it is important to use their last name when you do it. Hospitality also is about knowing your guests' preferences. Do they have a favorite table, favorite drink, favorite foods? You also need to know their hot button items, such as short lunch or long lunch, formal or informal, and whether to keep their water glass full or away from the table. Great hospitality is not just being friendly. It is about understanding the needs of the guest and being respectful to those wishes.

Let's review how hospitality fits into the worlds of quick service, fast casual and casual dining. In many cases, today's consumer is not looking for a great deal of hospitality. They are looking for convenience. When you look at the number of restaurants popping up where you order from a machine, you are not judging the restaurant on traditional hospitality. These customers want it easy and their order executed to their specifications. In these cases, hospitality can be very basic although it will still be critical to the overall experience. A proper greeting is essential. It does not have to be drawn out, but the guest should feel that you appreciate their business. It now comes down to exceeding expectations. Beyond the food, it is the friendliness of the staff who takes and delivers the orders.

Chick-fil-A stands out to me as a quick-service restaurant that exceeds expectations in terms of hospitality. The ordering process is efficient, the cashiers are friendly, and the manager is typically very active in the process. There is a clear presence that they are on top of things. The order is then delivered to your table and the staff is trained to ensure that your experience is a good one. The food is good for quick service, but it is the hospitality that brings me back when I am looking for a fast and easy option.

**Hospitality involves understanding your guests
and customizing to their needs.**

Key Takeaways: Hospitality: Beyond the food

"It is becoming increasingly difficult to differentiate yourself based solely on your food. Providing different elements of great hospitality can have a major impact on creating buzz and bringing your customers back."

1. **Hotel mentality for your restaurants**
   - Make sure that your brand focuses on the experience even if there is one thing that stands out every time a guest comes in, orders take-out, has it delivered or orders catering.
   - Avoid the term, "How was everything." It says nothing about really caring. Be specific. For example, "Did you enjoy the brick chicken? It has become one of our top menu items."
   - Encourage your customers to provide feedback. They really enjoy communicating with you and having a positive impact on what you do.

2. **Overcome a food quality issue with great hospitality**
   - What is your standard for handling a food quality issue?
   - Make a negative into a positive.
   - Not charging for the item is a given, but it is not enough to bring them back.
   - Develop standard operating procedures for your team.

3. **How do you exceed expectations in your restaurants?**
   - What is different about your brand that makes it memorable?
   - What about your service stands out?
   - Does your team really care about the guest?
   - Is your brand consistent location-to-location and day-to-day?

4. **Your favorite neighborhood restaurant has great elements of hospitality**
   - Think about what brings you back to your favorite restaurants.
   - Does the owner know you by face or name?
   - Is there an aroma that is memorable?

- Is there a twist (bread or accompaniment) that you talk or think about?

Simply being nice to people in a pressure filled world can stand out and make a tremendous difference in a guest's experience. Some areas of our country expect it and other parts of the country are surprised by it. Make it part of your brand's DNA and you will see your sales rise.

PART FOUR:

THE LIGHT AT THE END OF THE TUNNEL

25

TIME TO GET AN OUTSIDE LOOK

Restaurant people are so critical of other restaurants. Every detail is looked at when they go out to eat. The expectations are through the roof and the potential for not being fully satisfied is extremely high. You may even go into that restaurant looking for problems and may be happy that the food or experience was not good. This has a lot to do with your passion, creativity and desire to be the best. It also points to a potential issue of over rating your own operations while you underrate others.

I was trained very early in my career to focus on detail. I learned to look at my own operation with a clear focus and train my team accordingly. At that time, I was responsible for one restaurant or a small number of foodservice operations under one roof. Overseeing a brand with multiple restaurants or multiple concepts has a significant number of obstacles. For my first six years in the hospitality industry, I worked six days per week. One of my positions early on was as the general manager of a five-star restaurant. This truly was a great restaurant with great food and service. There was a four week wait to get a reservation with no end in sight. When I took over the responsibilities as general manager, it was already a great restaurant, so my concern was to make sure that that didn't change while I was in charge. My employer sent me out on my day off to a different five-star restaurant every week. It was a great perk for me, but also an assignment to see what they were doing well. I was there to experience how they did things and what made them successful. I could knit pick all I wanted, but they were a five-star restaurant too. My focus, ultimately, was to learn to keep focused on my own restaurant.

My hotel then put together a "visiting experience" program where someone from another hotel would come to my restaurant to do a critique based on the overall guest experience, starting from the reservation through to the end of the meal. I would not know when they were coming and vice-versa. I was lucky enough to be able do some of these critiques as well at other hotels. This was not meant to be a bashing, or attempt to get someone in trouble. It was an exercise to see what the guest was experiencing and how the information could help make the operation stay consistent and improve. An anonymous report was sent within two weeks of the visit, which I reviewed in detail personally and then with my team. Initially, I worried about when these reviews were taking place as I was being evaluated. Eventually, I looked at every customer as the potential reviewer. This improved my focus and allowed my team and I to treat all our guests in the same top-notch way.

When I transitioned into growing restaurant brands, there were a whole new set of obstacles, especially since I was incredibly protective of the recipes, systems and pretty much everything else. I spent as much time as I could in the restaurants, but gradually more of my time was spent on expansion. I was relying more and more on my key team members, but were the standards still where they needed to be? I decided to go back to what I learned in the hotel business. I needed to bring in someone with my passion and attention to detail, who did not have any hidden agenda. I also had to make sure that I was ready to see some things that would be difficult at first, but constructive in the end. More important, I needed to get my team aligned because this exercise was not to spy on them. We were doing this to keep all of us focused on getting better. I met with a group of my industry friends and acquaintances to discuss a strategy to work together to help improve each other's brands. None of us were direct competitors. Each brand developed their own report template and identified which locations would be visited for a full day. Reports were sent in two weeks later. The results were very similar to what I experienced in my early hotel days. And the outside look really helped me and my team focus.

After moving into the world of supporting restaurant brands, I quickly learned that if I could not get an operator to open-up and lower their barriers, there would no chance to support them as a partner. If you are looked upon as an outsider or third-party, you will never get the complete results that you were hired for. I can tell you that most restaurant brands are incredibly secretive and not only do not want help, they don't think they need help. In many cases, these are great brands with smart and creative leadership who have had great success regionally and are now growing or had great success at one time. They did not continue to re-invent themselves and therefore saw sales begin to drop.

When you are running into a pattern of flat or dropping revenue, rising costs, lack of infrastructure and in general, issues that are standing in your way of success, it is time to bring in someone from the outside. This is your brand and simply hiring someone with a great reputation or someone that claims that they have the miracle cure is not the way to go. The relationship is the key as there needs to be the potential of a partnership based on trust.

When you bring in a person from the outside, you need to make sure that they are working for you and not a specific manufacturer, distributor or grower. There can be no hidden agenda which would cloud their thinking. I would ask lots of questions and make sure you are satisfied with the answers. Once the person or organization is hired, you and your team will then need to have open dialogue and an open exchange of ideas. The final decision always rests with you so it almost does not need to be mentioned. Saving money is easy when you bring in poor quality products to replace quality products. A good partner would never allow that to happen, but will understand that that a sample could come in that is not up to the quality or specification that you provided. Sometimes a spec from manufacturer-to-manufacturer is simply not a match. You do not have to accept the change. Listening to options and understanding what is going on in the rest of the industry is powerful. Listening does not cost you anything and it guides you to looking at more opportunities.

Running and growing your business is very tactical. You need an offense and a defense and the ability to plan for both. Having smart, talented people with an open mind can provide you with great support.

Is your back door propped open? Is your walk-in cooler propped open?

Are their food safety issues? Do the tomatoes match your spec?

Key Takeaways: Time to get an outside look

"In many cases a secret, proprietary idea or recipe is either not new anymore or the people who you tell about it, really have no desire to use it or tell anyone about it. It becomes really important in the growth of your organization to begin to trust other people."

1. **Be as critical of your own brand as you are of others**
    - When you go to a restaurant and find all kinds of problems, be sure to consider what others are thinking of your restaurants.
    - Ask your friends (not restaurant people), to go to one of your restaurants for a meal and fill out a survey that will provide you with key information.

2. **It is not only important to get an outside look from someone else, but for you and your team to look at others**
    - Assign your key team members a specific brand to review and have them write up what they do well and what they don't.
    - Be objective when evaluating your food and service. Do you really have the best burger?
    - Do a lot of blind tasting. How do you measure up?

3. **Getting better means listening to others so you can evaluate where you are on point and where you need to adjustments.**
    - Ask a lot of questions. Encourage people to tell you what they think.
    - Respond promptly to guest comments through social media and your website.
    - Do small focus groups with your regular customers?

4. **Defending your business at all costs could lead to no business at all**
    - Evaluate your business regularly. How emotional are you to certain elements of your brand?

- Even if you have brought in someone from the outside to support you, if you do not open-up and allow them to do their job, you will get little benefit from the relationship.
- None of us are great at everything. We need others to provide us with their areas of expertise to make us whole.

The beauty of getting an outside look is that you have an opportunity to work with smart industry specialists who can add a tremendous amount of knowledge and expertise to yourself and your team.

26

PENNY WISE, DOLLAR FOOLISH

At the end of a negotiation, it is not uncommon for each of the two parties to feel that they got the better of the negotiation. At the beginning of the process, goals should have been set by both. Sometimes these goals are not reasonable and are simply set by one side feeling they have 'control" over the other and can get what they want. Other times, the goal is set based on the quickest way to get something done and that usually means a win for the other side.

There are many factors involved in purchasing. Some professionals really do their homework. They know the markets well. They speak to a lot of industry experts and have a good handle on where pricing could be both short term and long term. Do you lock in a deal long-term and get stability of pricing or play the market short term? They also will look at products from many manufacturers as quality, yield and other factors could impact the deal. You have a clear specification of an item and you need to be sure that the pricing you get matches your specification.

Everyone has their method, and in most cases, have a great deal of trouble adjusting to newer and more productive methods. Let's first look at old-fashioned traditional bidding, which is simply to have multiple options on the same product with no loyalty to anyone. This is very vanilla. If you have the best price, you get the business. This form of purchasing was what everyone used many years ago. This is an incredibly time-consuming process and not only does it cost you money with poor productivity, but it also increases your costs by beating everyone up. Yes, you pay more!

Let's say that you have three produce distributors and you get deliveries of produce three days a week to 10 locations. The produce distributors need to get their pricing to you by 3:00 p.m. each day, and then you have to alert your store managers as to who won the bid for the next day. Then, they must get their orders in to the produce distributors by 5:00.

The produce distributors then need to alter their delivery schedules based on whether they got the orders. They also must make sure that they have inventory on your products.

We will use tomatoes as the example. You are using 10 5x6 25-pound cases of tomatoes every other day for each location. The produce bid is therefore for approximately 100 cases or 10 cases for each of the 10 locations on their delivery. How badly does the produce distributor want the business? Do they stock the 100 cases in the hopes that they have the low bid or do they bid and, if they win, pick up the tomatoes at the produce market? The purchasing person, in most cases, will award the business with savings as low as .25 per case. What they don't realize is that each produce distributor is covering themselves in case they don't get the business. They will all be higher than the market so that they are able to make sure that they do not take a loss. They will also not be able to assure proper specifications all the time, as they are dealing with last minute notifications. In most cases, you will face wasted time, inconsistent specifications, lack of true distribution partners, and higher prices. In addition to that, you are playing the market on very volatile items. Teaming up with a produce-management company is essential when you dictate volume of over $1M in produce. They have direct deals with the growers and can minimize huge fluctuations in price and cap pricing when the market goes way up. They also can keep your specifications consistent by overseeing the produce distributor. In addition, they make ordering very simple for your restaurants and do price verification to make sure you are being charged properly. They will get a fee for each case (which they deserve to get) and you will save money and time.

Bidding out your broad-line distribution can really cost you money. When you do this, you are ultimately a street account. A broad-line distributor is focused on drop size. The larger the drop, the lower the mark-up. If your drop sizes are sporadic, you will pay significantly more for the mark-up. You may appear to pay less, but you are not. There are significant hidden costs that are buried in a distribution agreement. When you don't have a distribution agreement, it gets even grayer. The best thing you should do is have a professional negotiate your distribution agreement with a fixed-fee per case. Be sure to look at the entire agreement. That is where the hidden money is. A distributor is entitled to make money on your account, but not more than they should. I can tell you that I thought I negotiated some great distribution contracts as an operator and I did, if it was focused on mark-up alone. But, the key was that the distributor was making additional money on the landed cost before the mark-up was put on. As a consultant, I have looked at many distribution agreements where the mark-up was so low that the distributor would lose significant money. I want to assure you that distributors don't make deals with operators where they lose money.

Line item purchasing makes everything a commodity. Without question, buying power is a key component to better purchasing. Unfortunately, unless you are one of the big boys, your purchasing volume is not as much as you think it is. Consistency, including yield and shelf life, need to always be figured in with purchasing. If you are negotiating strictly on price, you could be getting older product, seconds or something which may vary from your specification. Beyond that, proteins vary considerably with the amount of fat and pump. With labor being an issue today as well as a food safety risk, you need to look much closer at what you are buying. In many cases, it costs you less to pay more. If you specified a seven-ounce chicken breast with a half-ounce of fat and, you had an employee who was prepping the chicken and was trimming the fat, as well as a half-ounce of chicken, you would end up with 6 ounces of useable chicken. I specifically had a client doing this that was a 100-unit chain. When the analysis was done, there was a $700,000 savings by spending more per pound for a clean, six-ounce breast. This is not unusual.

When it comes to purchasing, ask a lot of questions and always look for the right product. It is easy to be lulled to sleep on an item that has been used in your company for a long time, but things change, and therefore your brand may need to.

You got a great price on Blue Plate Mayonnaise, but did you really?

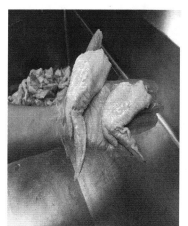

You may be paying a very low price for a raw random wing that is inconsistent in size, but are you really paying less? On the right is a consistent weight spec wing.

Key Takeaways: Penny wise, dollar foolish

"Buying power is a beautiful thing. Unfortunately, most brands simply do not have as much as they think they do. Line item purchasing, without looking at other factors, can potentially cost you significant dollars."

1. **The best negotiation is when both sides feel that they won**
   - Always know what your objective is before the negotiation starts.
   - Do not ask for the world as your negotiation may end at that point.
   - If you don't ask, you will never know, but be practical.
   - Know when you have maxed out. You need to look for the signs that you have squeezed everything out that you can.

2. **Stability of pricing in a long-term agreement may be the best way to go**
   - Evaluate how much time it takes to do short-term contracting.
   - Stable pricing allows you to do a better job of developing long-term menus and setting up budgets that are accurate.
   - Read as much as possible and talk to as many people as possible to understand the long-term markets before you lock in.

3. **Bidding is a time consuming and sometimes a costly way to purchase**
   - Short-term bidding will usually cost you money and time.
   - Be aware that if you use bidders all the time to lower the cost from your incumbent, ultimately others will not bid or they will bid high.
   - Build relationships with distributors and manufacturers that allow them to make what they should, but no more.
   - Have tools in place to keep everyone honest.

4. **Consistency, in most cases, outweighs the price of the raw product.**
   - Be sure to factor in labor, yield and shelf life.

- If you are a medium-sized company and are buying a specific product below the price of a larger-sized company, be sure to dig deeper before patting yourself on the back.
- Develop very detailed specifications to be sure that you are comparing "apples to apples."
- Do product cuttings and testing on everything, including your current spec products.

When you are short of time and lacking support, it is likely that you are making decisions which may not be in the interest of your organization. The price you are paying for the bottom 80% of spend may offset the great pricing you have negotiated on your top 20%.

27

PROTECTING YOUR JOB AT THE EXPENSE OF THE BRAND

I understand that everyone needs a job and wants to protect it, but don't you do that by doing a great job? As an executive responsible for a team of people, I always made it very clear what the expectations were of the company and then of them personally. There were always long-term and short-term goals. I have always had a daily to do list, weekly goals, monthly goals, quarterly goals, yearly goals, and then a three- to five-year goal. There were both financial objectives and operational ones to become better and re-invent when possible. I have always met with or spoke to each individual on my team at a minimum of every other week. I also had weekly department head meetings and full team ones. Beyond that, I always had an open-door policy. If team members didn't understand something or needed help, they could ask, and it was my responsibility to support them.

I worked for people at the beginning of my career and as an executive later. The culture starts at the top and funnels down to other supervisory people, and then to the rest of the team. Every team member, including high-level management, needs communication. It does not have to be frequent for many, but for some, constant communication is required. There should be quarterly reviews and very detailed written reviews each year. Every employee also should do a self-assessment at that time and review it with their managers. If their supervisors did a good job, then the employee self-assessment should match their manager's feedback. This is important to me because I once worked for a person who simply did not communicate. There was never a review and very little interaction. It was all about the yearly budget and driving the bottom line to benefit them.

At the end of the year, the financials were reviewed and there was a discussion about why something happened, whether it was positive or negative. Negatives were discussed at length and the positives were rarely addressed. There was a major disconnect with what happened during the course of the year because of poor communication. The effect was that end-of-year discussions were based strictly on numbers and not reality. I dreaded these end-of-year discussions because despite my best efforts, my tone would be negative. Negativity usually produces poor results. It also sometimes forces people to make bad decisions to make the boss happy. I would never do that, but I am going to tell you some real stories of that happening.

In many of these examples, there was a high-level executive who had a long-term employee. Therefore, the executive spent most of their time putting out other fires while expecting this employee to do the great job they had always done. Stability and longevity were viewed as the key to them doing a great job. However, in all of the cases below, it was just the opposite. It was about doing what you had to do to keep the boss distracted on anything and everything not related to them.

I was working on a produce program for a brand that used a tremendous amount of broccoli. This was a brand with significant volume in broccoli because they were a Mongolian grill concept. They were buying their broccoli florets from their broad-line distributor in four, three-pound cases. I did a preliminary analysis that showed I could save them $300k per year by moving them away from broad-line to a local produce distributor. I also could save them $600k if they switched to an 18-pound bulk pack. Sounds like a no-brainer, but it wasn't. They first said that they were required to buy their broccoli from the broad-line distributor and could not make the change. My team looked at their agreement and we clarified that by moving the broccoli, they would have to pay more per case for everything else, which would cost them a total $100k. This was followed by excuse after excuse and finally we were told that they were going to stay with the broad-liner. A year later, I found out that the purchasing person had become friends with the broad-liner representative and had gone to him to lower the price to keep the business. Their new broccoli price saved $100k but they were really losing $500k. The purchasing person told the boss that they had negotiated a $100k savings on broccoli. The boss was thrilled with the performance.

Another one of my clients was based in the Southeast and owned and operated 6 brands throughout the country. Their director of purchasing was based on the East Coast. They used a lot of shrimp and at one point, the shrimp market went through the roof. It was costing this company significant dollars and we were trying to help them bring their cost down. Their contract was expiring and the markets were starting to drop. Specifically, the long-term pricing projections were much lower. We were putting together shrimp contracts for multiple clients and were using the leverage to get the price down. We could secure a $.50 per-pound decrease and offered this to the purchasing person for this organization. He informed us that he had already secured a new deal. Shortly after, I saw that he had secured a $.25 per-pound decrease. I spoke to the CFO at corporate and asked whether he knew about this. He said that he only knew that the purchasing person had saved him a ton of money and he had praised him for it. He now realized that it had cost the company money. The purchasing person simply wanted credit as opposed to the best results for the organization.

In another case, we were working for a 100-unit Italian chain where the corporate chef was hiding from reality. This company was having food cost problems and was calling themselves a scratch kitchen, which could not have been further from the truth. They were making some things from scratch that they shouldn't have been and buying frozen items that should have been made from scratch. The chef was digging in his heels and would not adjust to our recommendations. The CEO loved the chef, believed that the food was great and determined that it was a purchasing issue. The purchasing person was replaced while the chef stayed employed. We also were told we were no longer needed. The concept went bankrupt nine months later.

There are so many stories like this. My belief is that you are doing a good job by understanding your strengths and weaknesses. It is not your fault that you are not perfect at everything or do not have the time, resources or buying power to get great results all the time. Working with others and being open-minded to opportunities that result in better top-line and bottom-line results for the company is what you are paid to do. You should be rewarded for this. Hopefully the culture of your organization would understand that.

You are paying $3 less per case for onions than anyone else. Your boss is impressed, but it is costing the company money.

Paying less and getting less. Paying more and getting much more.

Bulk broccoli could have saved $600k, but no interest?

Key Takeaways: Protecting your job at the expense of the brand

"Doing a great job is the best way to protect your job. Find a way to communicate with your boss on a regular basis and if you are the boss, be sure to communicate to your team. When a situation is created where a team member is measured in the wrong way, it may appear that they are doing a good job, but they may be costing you money."

1. **Setting Objectives for you and your team**
    - Accountability should be measured by the performance a person has accomplished, based on the agreed tasks that need to be completed.
    - Objectives change based on internal and external factors. It is essential to communicate with your team on a regular basis to adjust.
    - Formal reviews are crucial to both parties so they understand how they have done, how they are doing and where they need to go.

2. **The company's leader creates the company's culture**
    - If you communicate well and clarify expectations on a regular basis, then you have the right to hold the team accountable.
    - A great team will follow a great leader. If there is no leadership, they will treat their job focused only making money.
    - Learn to say thank you. Your team appreciates it more than you know.

3. **Long-term employees: Advantages and Disadvantages**
    - They may be loyal or they may be complacent.
    - They may send a great message to the rest of the team or they may send a bad message.
    - They may be taking advantage of you or possibly will protect you at all costs.

4. **<u>Why an employee will want to protect their job at the expense of the brand</u>**

- Their boss is a poor communicator and is simply interested in revenue or savings without asking a lot of questions.
- There is not a team oriented culture. Everyone is measured individually.
- There is high turnover in the company and simply showing some positive results will result in stability.

Results should always be measured. Whatever the results may be, there should be a written explanation which clarifies why something happened. You may not always like what you hear, but understanding the situation allows you to work closely with your team to strategize how the organization can always improve.

28

SELLING HOT DOGS AT THE FROZEN YOGURT STORE

They say that you can't put a square peg in a round hole. Selling hot dogs at the frozen yogurt store is a cry for help. We have all seen it. A restaurant or store that is trying too hard to drive new revenue and is really setting themselves up to lose revenue. Some of it is obvious. You have a sub shop with a loyal following. The menu is very traditional and has not been changed for years, and the place is known for having a quality product. A new burger concept opens a location right next door and you hear the food is great. Your sales are taking a hit and you feel you must react, but you make a bad decision. You add a burger to your menu and market it with a coupon that says buy one, get one free. You are getting some new business from a discount-oriented customer base and you are losing your loyal customers who simply wanted to try the new burger place. Your burger quality was mediocre and did not measure up to the restaurant next door, but they did not have subs to compete with you. This was your time to focus on your quality and service, and potentially run some new items that fit your strengths.

Discounting is dangerous to your brand, but if you are selling a commodity with no differentiation, you could lose based on price. If Southwest is running flights from New York to Chicago for $100 and American is at $200, who is going to get the business? Does American lower their prices to compete or stay at the same price? The answer is not as black and white as it appears. If Southwest was filling a plane with 200 people at $100, they would bring in $20,000. If American only had three-fourths of their plane full, they would bring in $30,000. Southwest would not be able to maintain the $100 price forever and America, by standing pat, may lose a few customers short term, but not long term. The same premise holds true with restaurants. Once you make the decision to be in the discount business, you become a discounter and it becomes very hard to change that.

McDonalds has done a fantastic job of providing discounted items on 'their terms." They introduced their "dollar menu" in order to drive more people into their restaurants. However, it accounted for about one-seventh of their business and lasted 11 years. At a certain point, they understood that they could no longer make money with this program and changed it. Today, McDonalds features certain items on a discounted menu, but most of their customers order from the regular menu and are encouraged to add fries and a beverage to provide value. They know what to discount and what not to. They also understand what is profitable and what is not. Virtually giving away coffee to get customers in to buy breakfast is strategic. Sure, they would love to get full price for the coffee, but driving customers into the restaurants is key. They also want them drinking their coffee. Their coffee is not always free and customers will get used to it and want it on a regular basis. McDonalds has positioned themselves to have items at a discount, but not everything. They also run specials at specific times, so it is understood that it is a special and will not be offered forever. By doing that, the customer understands that they either take advantage of it now or miss out on the opportunity. Once you prolong a discount or a special, you are de-valuing the item, which precludes you from offering it for a regular price in the future.

Now, back to the yogurt shop! When a yogurt shop starts selling hot dogs, this tells me that they are in trouble and that yogurt alone will not keep them in business. It also makes me wonder why they didn't think about other food options prior to opening the business. This could have been in the form of birthday cakes, ice cream, custard, candy, cookies, and other novelties made with yogurt in the middle. There are a lot of creative ways to create brand buzz while sticking to your roots.

There is no reason that a burger concept can't have healthier options such as turkey or vegetarian burgers. They also can create excellent salads or grain bowls to balance out the burgers. Many people love burgers and you want them to bring in others who may not want a burger. I look at it as the steakhouse that has fresh, high quality fish. If you are going to have it on the menu, it can't be an afterthought. The consumer today will see right through it. Prior to McDonalds expanding their menu to include salads, smoothies and other healthier items, they licensed six locations from Fresh City along toll roads and at airports. My brother and I really valued that relationship and respected the fact that McDonalds, at that time, knew that they needed to come up with healthier options, but were not ready for it. They therefore knew that Fresh City was all about fresh and that by having Fresh City right next to McDonalds, they could bring in revenue from parents and the kids who wanted other options. While we had to adjust to turn our 4,000-square-foot prototype space into an 800-square-foot space, we could not hurt the brand by sacrificing quality to accomplish this. These locations proved to be successful both for McDonalds and Fresh City.

Great operators stick to what has made them successful, but they continue to re-invent themselves. If you are a pizza concept, you have an opportunity to expand by offering non-traditional pizzas and other items related to that food category. If burritos are the latest craze, you can develop pizzas around those ingredients. If wraps are popular using tortillas or pita bread, develop wraps using pizza dough. This brings me back to the casual dining pizza chain that I once consulted for. They started as a pizza concept and before long they were serving steaks and, ultimately, making fresh desserts on site. The concept became confusing and watered down. The thing that I never understood was why they were not taking advantage of that delicious pizza dough that they made at each location. Why weren't they using it to make breadsticks and calzones, and all kinds of other creative items. They had become the yogurt shop selling hot dogs and it was confusing their customers and decreasing sales in the process.

Look at your strengths and build on those strengths. That is what made you great in the first place. When you focus on change based on competition, trends and forward thinking, be sure to never lose touch of where you came from.

Key Takeaways: Selling hot dogs at the frozen yogurt store

"When you go to a diner and see that big menu, you always wonder how everything can be good there. They really have no specialty, but the consumer accepts that they have a little of this and a little of that. For pretty much everyone else, you become known for something and need to make sure that you don't wander too far from what got you there."

1. **Don't react to competition after the fact**
    *   Be aware of where competition is coming from and study their menu, read their reviews and taste their food if possible.
    *   Spend extra time on training your team so that they are doing a first-class job.
    *   Evaluate your food and beverages and make sure products are up to standards.
    *   Work on a plan to stay relevant in preparation of another concept opening up nearby.

2. **Discounting can be dangerous**
    *   Avoid coupons unless you are desperate.
    *   Understand that once you discount an item, it becomes harder for the consumer to pay regular price later.
    *   Have certain items, including blue plate specials, that provide an exceptional value and keep everything else at regular pricing.

3. **What message does a customer get when you are selling hot dogs at the yogurt shop?**
    *   You are desperate to get additional business.
    *   The hot dogs are likely not going to be great as your business was not built to sell hot dogs.
    *   You are not focused on what you are doing well. You are looking for an easy fix.

4. **Focus on what you do well and stay current and innovative**
    *   Keep your products great and innovate and keep innovating.

- Be sure to add menu items that are of the same quality standards as your core items.
- Understand what is trendy and figure out how to incorporate.

Think of your brand the way you would when you go out for pizza, burgers or some other ethnic food. Would you order burritos at a Chinese restaurant? Would you order Peking ravioli at a Mexican restaurant?

29

HOW ARE YOU VIEWED BY YOUR PEERS, TEAM AND CUSTOMERS?

How you project yourself starts very early in your career. It leads to faster promotions, better locations to work at and credibility in the industry. Our goals vary considerably as professionals. Some want to make it to the top and will do anything to make it there. Others want to be politically correct and may have the same goals, but will be more methodical in their approach. How you communicate will dictate how you are viewed by others. In some cases, you may be viewed poorly despite your best efforts to do things right. This may be the result of someone simply not agreeing with your style. Nothing is perfect in how you are judged or how you judge people. The most important thing is to be a good listener and then communicate to others with a complete understanding. Where you get in trouble is when you communicate too quickly and without knowing all the facts.

Let's first look at your peers. In the hospitality industry, there is a common bond that exists in that everyone is fighting the same battle to success. You would think that restaurant executives would be great communicators, but in many cases, they are not. It is easy to fall into a me first mentality as you have a business to run, and in today's world may have private equity or financial institution partners. You are therefore under a microscope all the time. You can easily fall into only communicating with people if there is an advantage to you. Yes, you are busy, but at one time, you needed others to help you get to where you are today. Your peers deal with many of the same issues that you do. I have always valued the time and communication with others where we both could generate something to help us professionally and personally. Do you respond to e-mails or LinkedIn invitations from other foodservice professionals? How do you feel when you send an invitation or e-mail to someone and they simply don't respond? I always tell people that it would make me feel better if they told me to go jump off a cliff instead of simply just ignoring me. At least I would know how they felt. Personally, I always respond to industry professionals, even if it is a quick sentence. They deserve that and even if it is not what they want to hear, they will respect that you acknowledged them.

I belonged to a country club for a number of years and met some of my best friends there. Without question, people are very different from each other and you are drawn to the ones that are more like you. I am someone who, despite my differences, will always be cordial to others. Does it really hurt to say hello to people as you pass them? Is it too difficult to say thank you to the staff member who is working to make your experience better? I still can't believe the number of people who turned their head when they walked toward me at the country club. I guess I was not good enough for them. These also are the same people who will be overly friendly to you if they want something, but will turn their back if you have nothing to give them. Most of the time, you can see right through these people. I had a situation at Fresh City where I started doing business with a vendor and specifically with one of their salespeople. I did business with that person and company for 25 years and I built up a trust with this individual. When I sold Fresh City in 2011, he did not need me anymore for the business and he stopped communicating. It turned out to be a 25-year sales job. I usually can see right through these things, but I was completely caught off guard on this one.

Leadership of your staff can be done in different ways. I believe that you win or lose as a team. I always communicate to my team and work hard to make them better personally and for the good of the company. To some, I was a micro manager, but in my view, I was just a manager providing direction and support. Most people want guidance and the ability to contribute. I believe in these people and I always listen to them and allow them to be a big part of my success. The I vs. We mentality is one that really sets us apart. We all need to look out for ourselves and our families first, but we should recognize the people who are working hard on our behalf. No matter what business I am the leader of, I always talk in terms of we. There are few businesses where you can be successful on your own. I appreciate the people who work hard on my behalf and I thank them for it. I also make them accountable for what they do and they thank me for that. When Fresh City won awards, or when I wrote articles or spoke at conferences, I always mentioned my team. When a picture was taken of me for an award, I brought other key team members into picture. I also have witnessed the opposite: successful leaders who made it about them rather than the team. This is not the type of company culture that many want to be around. It does not take much to recognize others.

How about your customers, business neighbors, vendors, and others? If you are nice and respectful, you can be strong and tough in business with no repercussions. To this day, I have an excellent reputation with manufacturers. When I see them at conferences, we joke about the good old days when I was "beating them up" to get the best price. They still tell me that they had great respect for me because I told them what I wanted and when I needed it. In return, I responded to them professionally even if they were not awarded the business. Just because you are in a position of strength, does not mean that you need to treat people poorly.

I also believe that you should be active in the business community in every market you are in business. Support schools and athletics. Give back where you can. It is important that much of this comes from the heart and from trying to do the right thing. I also visit Cornell each year to speak at a class, provide internships for students and answer their questions via e-mail. Giving money to your school is great, but it is impersonal. It is important to make a difference for the future of our industry.

One important thing in terms of your customers is to do what you say. Why put something on your website where guests can communicate issues if you have no intention of responding? It clearly says that you don't care. I avoid those brands like the plague. No one tries to do a mediocre job, but if they work to improve, I support them.

Success requires a great team!

Key Takeaways: How are you viewed by your peers, team and customers

"The way that you communicate will be the way that you will be perceived by others. It is easy to see who is humble and who is arrogant. We all want to make it to the top, but we need to make sure we acknowledge the people who got us there."

1. **Getting to the top by stepping on top of people or stepping with people**

- Industry leaders are driven to make their brand great so it can grow.
- Nobody can get to the top on their own!
- Even when you make it to the top, you can quickly come back down to earth. It gets hard when you reach out for help and no one is there.

2. **Treat your peers with respect. You can learn from each other**

- Seek out others who you can collaborate with. Not everyone is a direct competitor.
- Your brand is not as good as you think and your competitors are not as bad as you think.
- Be careful what you say and who you say it to.

3. **Grow your business as a team and recognize them as you gain success**

- Remember that you are not an expert at everything. A successful organization requires great people.
- Communicate strategically with your team. Give them guidance and allow them to succeed, even if they make mistakes.
- Do not take all the credit for your company's success. Recognize the people who helped you get there.

4. **Listen to what others say and then provide your thoughts**

- Encourage your staff to offer their thoughts on how your business can constantly improve.

- Listen to your customers. They want to be your partner and are trying to help. Don't ignore their feedback.
- Despite the great things you have done with your brand, have thick skin, and be prepared to adjust.

You never know when you will need the support of someone else. Be careful not to burn bridges and treat people as you would want to be treated yourself. Regardless of your position or status, you can learn from others and you can make a difference in the lives of others.

30

PROTECTING YOUR BRAND: ADJUSTING TO OUTSIDE ISSUES

You work on your brand and you open to rave reviews. You tweak and tweak again, and then you decide to grow the brand. Growth may be a combination of company locations, franchise or licensed locations. But with it comes a whole new set of issues. You must prepare early for growth in your core market in to avoid the pitfalls that will come from entering new ones.

One of the franchisee areas for Fresh City was Virginia. We had signed a master franchise agreement for that market and the first location appeared to be a great one. We were in multiple markets by this time, but with each new market we encountered some of the same issues. No matter how many locations you have, when you go to a new market, you become an independent again. You will need a distributor to deliver your spec products and a produce distributor to do the same. They may be a division of Sysco or US Foods, but to them you are a royal pain. They need to bring in the items for you and need to worry about some of the products' shelf lives. You and your team also are looking at yourself as much bigger than you really are, and that attitude is not appreciated by the distributor. You need to be prepared to sub out certain products that come close to your specification as your low volume items will be an issue. Be aware of what those items are and work on a contingency plan well before it becomes a problem.

Another major factor is that the consumer in your new market may not be familiar with your brand. Just because you are loved in your core market doesn't mean that customers will be waiting for you to open in a new one. Know your competition extremely well. Understand the customer base and what they are eating and drinking. Over time, I learned about regional taste preferences. In New England, I grew up with medium rare roast beef. Consumers in virtually all other markets across the country like their roast beef medium-well. I remember the Virginia staff saying that the roast beef was "raw." It was a lesson learned and, as we grew, I continued to learn about the differences in each market. Once you figure out the market, build up the hype early and often. Have tastings and focus groups to get the consumer to buy in. Don't just open the doors and expect a line.

When I was with Hyatt, early in my career, I spent about six to eight months at each location and then was transferred. I grew up in Boston and went to school in New York so I was used to a very fast-paced lifestyle. I started with Hyatt in Orlando, Fla., then went to Los Angeles, Chicago, Boston, and finally, Hilton Head Island, S.C. Each market was completely different and the expectations of the staff had to be adjusted. When I got to Hilton Head Island, I was extremely naïve. I was my usual intense personality and was extremely cordial to my staff, but my demands were unreasonable. The pace was so much slower there and it was up to me adjust my pace. I just needed someone to tell me and my boss did. It was quite simple, but was hard for me to understand at first. I was used to something else entirely and had been my whole life. When you grow your company into a new market, understand how your employees work and what your customers expect. In some markets, people are more laid back and can be extremely nice. They expect to be treated in the same way. It does not mean that they are lazy. When you send your training team out to hire and train, they should understand the various personalities in each market and how to adjust their methods to them.

There also are factors that are quite different from market to market. Weather is a major one. While snow and cold may affect you in New England, there is heat in the south and southwest, while hurricanes, tornados, and Santa Ana winds exist in other parts of the country. You need to understand that 1-inch of snow in Atlanta or Charlotte could shut the city down for the day. Therefore, you must plan accordingly for potential closed or delayed days. In addition, you should be aware of the importance of outside seating in warmer climate-areas. How long will you have this seating? Do you need heaters or misters? What about air conditioning? Your electrical costs will be more in an "extreme weather" market and your budget should reflect this.

The focus needs to always be about consistency. Having the proper infrastructure to support your growth is critical to your brand. I have seen so many brands accept standards in non-core markets that they would never accept in their core. When you franchise you brand, you can't make it so complex that it can't be duplicated anywhere else in the country. There are certain ingredients and products where your specification can closely be duplicated and the customer would not have a bad experience. But, if your brand promotes the best chili, pesto or sausage, and you need to substitute an inferior product in a market, you will quickly lose business and your reputation.

I also see some franchise locations using non-logo paper products while corporate locations are all brand focused. Packaging needs to be consistent. Sometimes you can get, nationwide, environmentally friendly products that includes a brand message on the package. This could be a better than just using your logo. Pick your spots and be consistent. Having a strong traveling team is crucial to the brand. They need to be extremely detail oriented and know how to teach in a way that aligns your team members in every market. They need to buy-in to doing it right because they want to instead of because they have to.

Competition and potential competition also must constantly be looked at in each market. There are some fantastic concepts in every market. They are not all national brands, but some will become them. Others will remain as independents or become regional chains. Some innovative companies will have multiple concepts within one market. The simple question to your team or franchisees in each market is: "What is new in your market that we should be reviewing?" Everyone needs to stay on their toes. They need to go eat at the competition and listen to what the customers are saying. If something is great and people are loving it, you need to know what it is and put it on your development list, not only for that market, but possibly for your entire company.

When you are busy, someone else wants a piece of you. They will try to open near you and copy as much as possible what you do well. Protect your brand by being proactive. Understand each market before committing to it. Once you make the commitment, choose great locations and dig deep into the market to make sure you are ready to open the doors. Be sure to always enjoy your success and be vigilant about your "what's next" approach. Nothing is forever, unless you are constantly re-inventing.

One day you are the only show in town and
then a competitor opens next to you.

You have a unique product and then others
copy it. What is your next move?

Key Takeaways: Protecting your brand: Adjusting to outside issues

"There are so many outside issues that can and will affect your business unless you always remain on guard and prepare for the next phase of your business. Take the time to understand what is going on around you and plan accordingly."

1. **A new market means that you are temporarily back to be an independent**

   - Limit your proprietary items in your core market and be prepared to have approved subs until you grow a new market.
   - Build a relationship with your distributors in each market. You are not important to them based on your volume in another market.
   - Build a great team immediately. The buzz that your new employees will create will have a great impact when you open.

2. **Do not expect the consumer in a new market to know who you are**

   - Don't assume that your success as a regional brand will translate to consumers in a new market waiting for you to open.
   - Educate the new consumer on who you are and what makes you different.
   - It is essential to create a buzz that involves getting your new customers to try your food well before you open.

3. **New competition can come quickly**

   - Do not be fooled by long lines and great sales.
   - A direct competitor will be watching you and will open right next to you without thinking twice.
   - Do everything you can on your lease to eliminate as much competition within the landlords control.

4. **A signature menu item can be knocked off**

- If a menu item is special and is attracting customers to your restaurant, others will find a way to knock it off.
- While others are trying to duplicate your best items, you can be working on your next great products.
- Don't limit your signature items to one category. You do not want to be pigeonholed as a one-trick pony.

The effort needed to keep your brand on top never ends. It is easy to lose focus of this when you are seeing success. The "what's next" mentality is crucial to protecting your brand.

31

THE POWER OF NETWORKING

I find it very unusual that many brands do not send their team to industry events. Staying current requires people to get away from their world for a short time in order do a tremendous amount of listening and thinking. To this day, I get more done on an airplane than anywhere else. Sure, there is e-mail to distract you, but being able to focus without constant interruptions is actually a breath of fresh air.

It is true that some events tend to be more social than business. Those are the ones to stay away from and regardless of which events you go to, it is up to you and your team to set the parameters of what you want to accomplish. When I put together my budget for each year, I always included a certain expense for conferences, trade shows, networking events and prospecting. I brought my team together to review each of the potential events and reviewed why they felt there was a potential for success. Questions to consider included how many people should attend, who should go, how much time should be spent there and what the cost was associated with each event. If someone from your team goes to an event, they should come up with a game plan. This should include putting together a clear agenda with a target list of people to meet with or products to look at. At the end of each event, there also should be a summary put together with a follow-up plan of action.

For the most part, getting operators to these events is the focus of the event organizers. The manufacturers, distributors and consultants are the ones who pay for these events, so you are very much in demand. You have no obligation to meet with these people and even if you do, you are not obligated to use their products or services. You can talk to them for five minutes or five hours. You really control that. The key is to ask a lot of questions and to learn as much as you can. Without question, if you are prepared, you will take a tremendous amount of information back to your company and if you don't, you will cross the event off your list.

Should you have someone go to the National Restaurant Association Show? The answer is absolutely. I never missed a year as an operator and always went looking for two new things that could make a difference for my brand in the coming year. By walking the floor, you could see all the newest products and services that were being promoted. I also met with key manufacturers and other partners. What a great way to discuss my growth plans and negotiate some potential new deals. I also set up meetings with franchisees and others. I brought certain key people with me and we spent quality time strategizing. In addition, I set up part of a day to visit five concepts that I felt we could learn from visiting. Many operators go every other year and do not send the right people. Companies tend to look at this as a bonus for someone to go. I never thought of it that way. I always looked at it as an opportunity to network and get business done in a high energy environment. Regarding regional trade shows, there is no cost except for time. It is a good opportunity to send a couple of people who typically would not go to a national event, but they would need to be well prepared and accountable for follow up.

There some excellent events specific to CEOs, CFOs, supply chain, and culinary personnel. Many of these are paid for by the organizers. Some of these are roundtable forums where you can sit with others who are in the same shoes as you and compare notes. Some events allow you to be a speaker or to be on panels. This provides you with exposure to the industry. Certain supply chain events such as Market Vision, allow purchasing professionals the opportunity to work on contracts, learn about commodity forecasts and spend time with other professionals like themselves. The same holds true for your culinary team. Getting them together with other culinary professionals will make them better at what they do. Manufacturers always welcome operators to visit their companies and to spend time in the kitchen working on new and innovative ideas, and they cover all the costs.

There are other "major" industry events that provide great opportunities to network. Conferences like Restaurant Finance and Restaurant Leadership are must-attend events, but only if you use them to your advantage. I worked these events both as a chain operator and as a cost reduction consultant. I never had a bad meeting as an operator because I had filtered out the meetings based on who I wanted to see and what I wanted to accomplish. I had a key person from my team make sure I had a full schedule of quality meetings. I even made sure that if I went to a cocktail party or dinner that there was great potential for a quality outcome. I also always left time to visit a location or two if I had restaurants in that market. Setting up meetings as a consultant was quite a bit different. I narrowed down who I wanted to meet with and why. Contrary to what operators think, my time was valuable too, and I did not want to waste my time meeting with the wrong people. I always respected the operators who got back to me to find out what I wanted to accomplish and why they should meet with me. Having both sides prepared allowed for greater productivity at the meeting and less time allocated. If the meeting went well, we coordinated follow up.

I am a big believer in prospecting. In today's world, most prospecting is done electronically. You may know who is growing, what is going on in the market and much more, but you really don't have a feel for what is truly happening. To truly understand a brand, you need to spend time at their locations experiencing the food, service, ambiance, and systems. What makes this brand different and how can you incorporate some of their successes into your concept? What you learn on these trips can keep you and your team focused on always trying to get better.

If you are going to invest in networking, you need to send the right people and have a plan to maximize your investment. Time is your biggest investment and you want to maximize every minute of every trip to the fullest. There should be business, education and time to socialize to come back to your business with the excitement level needed to move your business forward.

Restaurant Finance: So many opportunities to accomplish great things.

Restaurant Leadership: Networking with Peers.

National Restaurant Association Show:
There must be something there.

Key Takeaways: The Power of Networking

"Networking provides you with an opportunity to ask questions and listen to what other industry experts have to say. This information allows you to evaluate how you can keep your brand moving in a direction that will keep it vibrant and on top for many years."

1. **Plan your schedule and your team's schedule a year in advance to have the opportunity to network**
   - Periodically getting out of your world for a short time can help you look at things differently.
   - Certain events will provide you and your team with the opportunity to meet multiple manufacturers, franchisees and others, which will save you considerable time.
   - You always have the option to cancel or make changes to a schedule.

2. **Develop a budget for events each year that you can stick with**
   - Key members of your team should submit any events that they feel would be beneficial along with a budgeted cost.
   - Many events are free for operators. You should always ask for the world as event planners want operators there.
   - Be smart with what you spend. It is not always necessary to stay at the 5-star resort.

3. **Have a strategy going into each event. Planning will result in success**
   - Try to get industry visibility while there. Getting on panels can really help your business.
   - Each event should be justified both in cost and time. Whoever is going should have a clear agenda and then a follow up strategy.
   - Everyone wants to meet with you and some of them you want to meet with, too. Be sure there is clear criteria to make the best use of your time.

4. **Take advantage of every travel opportunity.**

- Beyond going to a conference or trade show, take advantage of every minute wherever you are.
- Prospecting should be a part of every trip. It is a great opportunity to see brands that you hear about, but have not experienced.
- Visit your locations/franchisees when you are in their markets.

You can learn so much by being away from your home base for even a short period of time. Your peers have many of the same issues that you do and most of these people are looking for the same answers that you are.

PART FIVE:

FULL STEAM AHEAD

32

ARE YOU TRULY DIFFERENT?

Looking at things from both ends of the spectrum clarifies that most brands cheat a little bit on some of the things that make them different. At the same time, you may be doing some great things that differentiate you, but nobody knows it. If you want credit for something, execute what you say and without question, tell everyone that you are going above and beyond.

This whole book is about being different. Let's focus first on what you communicate regarding your food, service, culture, team, support of charities, environmental initiatives, and so much more. What is marketing vs. reality, and how much of this is what you want to be known for as opposed to what you really are?

Earlier, we touched on some "hot buttons" issues such as local, scratch cooking and environmental friendliness. Many of these "hot buttons" don't have an exact definition, so you can stretch them a bit. Others are much more black and white. There is so much pressure to be different and your customers are demanding a lot more, but we recognize that they are not willing to pay for it. You therefore need to be realistic about what you can and can't do. This involves proper positioning with a focus on doing what you consistently can do at each location all the time. If you say you use local tomatoes, you need to use local tomatoes year-round at every location. If that is not possible, you need to state that you use local tomatoes whenever available. This says that you try hard to do the right thing even though it may not be possible 365 days each year.

Think about it! What really makes you different from your direct competitors? Everyone thinks that it is their food. I have never heard an operator tell me that their food was not great, but is it different? What is memorable about your ingredients, preparation, presentation, flavor profile and perceived value? Specifically, what keeps your customers coming back? We are all creatures of habit and when something wows us, we remain loyal. What are the key components that made us loyal and more important, what has kept us loyal? Did a new brand come in to your market and do something different that changed your habits?

Six months ago, a new coffee brand came to the Boston area and I checked it out as I would with any new brand. I was pleasantly surprised by the quality of the coffee drinks as well as the food that was offered. Furthermore, the environment was highly conducive to doing business as it was extremely comfortable and inviting. Ultimately, I changed my habits and start my day there almost every day. I meet people for meetings there. The staff knows me and understands how I like my expresso drink prepared. Most of all they have been consistent. Their differences lured me in, but staying consistent kept me there.

At Fresh City, we worked extremely hard to have some organic products, some environmentally friendly products, and so on. We made a big deal out of those items and made sure that customers knew which of those items fit those descriptions. I identified the local produce items that were used in our salads and stir fry. We also incorporated and communicated the use of organic ingredients, such as black beans, into our burritos. We used antibiotic free chicken, eco-friendly packaging where we could, and we tried not to use bleached or white products. Customers really do appreciate that you are making a concerted effort to do what is right. You simply need to communicate with them and make it a major initiative to keep trying to do more. As a consultant, I went into many brands that were positioning themselves as doing things 100% of the time and using it as a differentiator. When I saw what was really going on, it was a disappointment. A customer will understand that if you have restaurants in Maine and you market local produce, you won't be able to get local produce 12 months per year. It is not possible. Meanwhile, it is almost expected if you are in California. Be transparent with what you do and your customers will be loyal.

Looking at it from the other side, are you doing some great things and not telling your guests? What is the point of doing something if you are not going to get credit for it? Let's say that you are purchasing fresh cod for your fish n' chips and on your menu, it just says fish n' chips. Could you be using pollock or swai instead of cod? I went through this exercise with many of my clients by doing a blind tasting using the three varieties of fish fried up in a delicious beer batter. In every case, it was difficult to tell the difference. Why should you spend the money on cod if your customer doesn't know about it or care?

If you truly are different, you should be recognized for it and charge a price that reflects it. If you are producing your soups from scratch, grinding your "fair trade" coffee in house, smoking your meats on premise, or roasting your turkey fresh in the kitchen, you need to market this to your customers and be consistent from location to location. If your customers don't know about it, rethink it. If you are doing these things and your competition is not, do what's necessary to make sure your customers take notice.

One of the goals at Fresh City was to make sure that the basics really stood out for our guests. This included our chicken soup, clam chowder and chili, Caesar and ranch dressings, chocolate chip cookies, tuna salad, Teriyaki sauce, and a few other items. These items were quite sensational and always consistent. We also built on the differentiators of our other more innovative products. However, the basics, when done right, can really create a buzz. To this day, people still ask me why our tuna salad was so great. That is an answer for another time.

It truly is a slippery slope and operators need to think hard about where they should put their efforts to differentiate. Your brand needs to stand out among the crowd for certain things that will be consistent, no matter when or where customers go to your restaurants. What is most important is that they know you really care about doing what is right and make every effort to seek out the best products for both them and the environment.

Fish n' Chips: This menu insinuates fresh with no commitment, and states, "We serve the freshest ingredients we can find."

The best sushi customized in front of you. One of my greatest experiences in food ever....

Key Takeaways: Are you truly different?

"Honesty and integrity are virtues which can help make a business successful. The key is to be focused on how you can always do better and make sure that your customers are actively involved. Every concept can and should tell the world about their exploits and how they will continue to work to improve. At the same time, they must be careful not to go over the top and deceive their customers."

1. **<u>Offer your guests what you can execute consistently.</u>**

   - It only takes one time, when a product has been altered in a negative way, for a guest to feel that you have changed your standards.
   - If you promise something, be sure that it is real.
   - Seasonality can't be a factor unless you are transparent about variability.

2. **<u>If you are doing something special, be sure to get credit for it</u>**

   - Your personal pride can be costly. If you go to great lengths to use or prepare products above and beyond, tell your guests.
   - Use social media and local publications to talk about these special differentiators.
   - Pick your spots. Sometimes you are doing special things that are costly and the guest does not see or know the difference.

3. **<u>Communicate to your customers and your team. They will respect you for it</u>**

   - Know your customer and work hard to give them what they are looking for.
   - Don't try to fool the people who hold the cards on your success.
   - Encourage open communication through surveys, focus groups and other sources.

4. **<u>Make sure your basics are excellent and can stand up to anyone</u>**

   - As you work on bold products that differentiate you from others, remember that the bulk of consumers still order the basics.

- If your basics are above and beyond, they can be used as bases that can be infused with bold flavors.
- In addition to promoting unique items, don't be afraid to promote certain standard items as must haves for your customers.

Consumers today are smarter than ever before. They can see through things that are not as advertised. When you promote something that is unique and different, be sure that you can execute it 100% of the time and at every location.

33

TRYING TO FIGURE IT OUT

I concluded, a long time ago that I will never figure anything out to perfection, and that is a good thing. The quest for getting better both personally and professionally should really drive us all. We need to celebrate our wins and successes and then move toward what's next. If you dwell too long on your successes, you become complacent and others will pass you buy.

I am lucky enough to have been a New England Patriots fan during their successful run of championships starting in 2000. As of 2018, they had won five Super Bowl championships. I have learned many lessons by watching them regarding to how to live my life and manage people. Every win the Patriots have accomplished, including the Super Bowl, was met with celebration for a job well done. Everyone who had anything to do with those wins deserved, at minimum, a pat on the back. After some rest, it was always time to focus on the next game. The Patriots had to focus on "one game at a time" in order to capitalize on their potential to win another championship game or Super Bowl.

Their focus and mindset reminds me of putting together a budget for the year that is also comprised of smaller, monthly budgets. Along with those budgets you had to put together a strategic plan that would give you the opportunity to meet your annual goal. Making or beating your numbers in January is important, but it is only a stepping stone to your yearly ones. If you have too big of a parade early in the year, you may take your eye off the ball and have a poor February or March, and this would put tremendous pressure on the rest of the year.

When I visit a restaurant that has a Best of Chicago plaque hanging in their window for 2010, 2011, and 2012, and it is now 2017, I wonder what happened. Was there too much celebrating going on and not enough self-assessment to continuously improve? As an outsider to this restaurant,

I would be curious as to what they were doing from 2010-2012 to make them stand out from others. Clearly, they had worked hard to figure out how to be recognized. As opposed to the Patriots, they were focused on the past and not on today or tomorrow. Their plaques may allow for great stories, but not for a sustainable business.

One of the terms I use all the time is, "don't start the parade until it is time." A big mistake that many make, is to make announcements before a deal is closed. This could involve a big real estate deal that is imminent or a catering job that has been verbally agreed to. The examples are endless. You may want personal recognition or you simply are having a meeting or filling out a report and want to make an announcement. I have seen so many examples where verbal agreements were never signed. Having the parade too soon reminds me of the tuba players at the front of the line in a parade. If they stop, everyone simply walks into them and falls over.

I remember in 1986 when the Red Sox were playing the Mets in the World Series. The Red Sox had not won a pennant since 1918 and were two strikes away with a lead. The scoreboard in New York said Congratulations to the Red Sox. Unfortunately, they had not won yet and of course, they blew it.

It took 18 more years for them to win.

In competition, whether business, sports or anything else, it is not over until the proper time. Everyone must focus on figuring out how to get to the finish line. A race is not won by taking the lead and coming up short at the end. You need to have a plan that focuses on a clear strategy. Do you have the right people in the right places? Are you listening to your customers/clients, or are you telling them what you think they want to hear? Do you understand what your competitors are doing to make sure that they are the ones winning and not you? Are you adjusting along the way to make sure you still can get to the finish line?

When I do a yearly review of my team, there are ratings for each category ranging from 1 for the best and 5 for the worst. During the first year of the review, I always explain that I don't give 1s. Even for myself. I truly believe that most people could be given a grade of 99 out of a 100 on something. That means they are very good at that function and would be characterized as a specialist. Does that mean that they are perfect and can't learn anything else? Challenging yourself and others to continually try to figure it out should be extremely motivational. We all need to make sure though that we never lose sight of rewarding and acknowledging people. Trying to improve all the time does not mean that you are not good at what you do. I thank the people who I work with all the time and you should too.

Many of us like to read books and quite a few of these books are part of a series with the same characters. I specifically read legal thrillers and mysteries. When we read or possibly watch a movie, we are trying to figure out how it will end. That is what keeps us coming back. If it is a series, I can't wait to read the next book. If it is a one-time book or movie, I may have figured it out or could have been totally surprised. If there is a finality to the book or movie, there is almost a let-down. We all like to be challenged in some way, some more than others.

In terms of the restaurant business, there are so many obstacles that need to be faced every day. You are dealing with the quest to get great people and keep them. The cost of food and other supplies is not constant and you have to be on top of the markets. Your customer base will fluctuate. What you have on day one will be altered by competition, traffic patterns, new residential or commercial tenants, and other obstacles that you may not have been prepared for.

By having a mentality of always trying to figure it out, you will continue to stay focused on what you need to do so you can be relevant in a business that has a high mortality rate. Taking your eye off your business for even the shortest time can lead to quick deterioration. Being in the hospitality industry already makes you a winner. Now, I want you to stay successful in it.

The parade was announced too early. The Red Sox lost the World Series in 1986 and had to wait another 18 years to win.

Finally won it all! It took a long time to fi

World Series celebration
Check out scenes from the celebration in St. Louis. (Globe Staff Photo / Jim Davis)

Sox win first Series since 1918

While church bells rang in small New England towns and horns honked on the crowded streets of the Hub, the 2004 Red Sox last night won the 100th World Series, completing a four-game sweep of the Cardinals with a 3-0 victory on the strength of Derek Lowe's arm. Playing 1,042 miles from Fenway Park, the Sox won it all for the first time in 86 long and frustrating seasons. (By Dan Shaughnessy, Today's Globe)

TODAY'S TOP SOX STORIES

- **GAME RECAP:** Possible dream
- **MACMULLAN:** Tears of joy
- **RYAN:** It was wild ride
- Nixon's gamers
- Theo's actions loud as words
- **SOX NOTEBOOK:** Now what?
- Most valuable in the clutch

Key Takeaways: Trying to Figure it out

"When the day comes that you feel you have it all figured out, put someone else in charge of whatever made you successful."

1. **The quest to get better**
   - This attitude breeds enthusiasm and excitement.
   - Everyone gets better when a team works together trying to figure out things what's next.
   - Be a great listener as some of the best ideas come from others.

2. **Don't start the parade until it is time**
   - It is a mistake to announce a win before you have completed the project.
   - Be very careful of verbal confirmations. They can blow up quickly.
   - Know the decision makers. Parades tend to start when you get an OK from someone who is not the final decision maker. Ultimately, this win may fizzle because of that.

3. **Get to the finish line**
   - Very few things are black and white, and there are obstacles along the way. Those need to be solved to achieve your goals.
   - Along the way, you must continue to push to the finish line. If it is deemed that getting there comes at too much of a cost and not enough reward, be prepared to stop.
   - Open-ended never works. There should be a clear path to the finish line on even the smallest projects.

4. **Being a specialist at everything?**
   - Great leaders hire great people who are better than they are at their area of expertise.
   - Some people may be at the very top of their specialty, but that does not guarantee that they will stay on top.

- While trying to figure out how to stay great at a specific function, we all need to figure out how to improve in areas that are not our strengths.

Great cultures are driven by people who are innovative. They celebrate their wins and learn from their losses, but most important, they leave them behind to focus on what's next.

34

DIFFERENT IS BETTER THAN BETTER: HOW TO KEEP YOUR BRAND CURRENT

The focus of the first 33 chapters of this book was to say that everyone who got to chapter 34 is doing a really good job. At the same time, I want to remind all of you (and me) that what comes next is how you will be viewed. I always look back at what I have accomplished to see if I could have done better. Really, what I continue to analyze is whether I could have done anything differently to make myself and the organizations that I was a part of, stand out from everyone else.

As a reminder, being better is all in the eyes of the beholder. Whether in competitive sports, academics, job performance or any other field, we have all felt that we were better in some way. However, there is a difference between confidence and arrogance. Confidence is so important on the road to success yet, it is unfortunate that many people have very little self-confidence. They may have the ability to make a tremendous difference, but never get the opportunity. On the flip side, there are many "blowhards." These are individuals who are over-bearing and pushy that temporarily go to the top despite having less talent. Eventually, their arrogance gets in the way in the same manner that lack of self-confidence does. We are all given gifts, yet how we use those gifts is up to each of us.

For example, I love music and watch on television some incredibly talented people with extraordinary voices. What really stands out when I listen to the judges is how they view the contestants. These contestants all have great voices or else they would not be on the show. It really comes down to what they do with that great voice. It needs to stand out in some way and if it is different enough, they have a chance to really make it in the industry.

Think about some of the great pitchers in baseball. Many great pitchers can throw 100 miles an hour. That is spectacular, but it does not guarantee success even if they do make it to the major leagues. Great competitors find a way to differentiate and that is through mixing up their pitches, disguising their pitches and finding a way to have movement on the ball and not straight fastballs. The pitchers are getting better, but so are the hitters. Throw them a 100 mile an hour fastball with no movement and they will hit it a long way.

The biggest obstacle continues to be after you have done something great. You may have been recognized by a critic or received an industry award. You are on top of the world and feeling that you really have done what it takes to be the best. As I stated before, enjoy it and take advantage of the notoriety, but use it as a stepping stone. The minute that you are recognized is when you go under the magnifying glass by your customers, the press and the hospitality industry. The expectations become much greater and the focus on standards begins to become less of a focus. Don't allow yourself or your team to become absorbed by your recognition. Your competition is still there and still feels that they are better than you. Now, they will work even harder to find a differentiator to prove it. They are going to go to the next level and try catch you sleeping.

We also all know that in our business, who you know is a factor in who gets an award, who gets press and who is given the opportunity to speak at conferences in front of industry professionals. I have been on both sides of this. If you do get a break, make sure that you realize it. Keep your ego in check and push hard to justify the opportunity. If you see someone else getting accolades and you believe that your brand is truly different, push hard to be recognized without getting into an "I am better" mentality. As an operator, I was given many opportunities to speak at industry events and I took advantage of each one. As a consultant, my opportunities were few and far between. Event organizers were aligned through friendships with other consultants, and even if they were not equipped to speak on a topic, they were given the opportunity. This made me realize the importance of working harder to make a strong statement, one that was different from everybody else. Look for ways to add value and your relationships will be long term. Stay complacent, and someone else will take away your business.

It is ultimately about who you are as a person. When you have integrity, and maintain this integrity for the long haul, you build a respect that lasts a lifetime. The culture of the team that works with you breeds the same respect from industry professionals. This is part of being different. You may be better than other operators or consultants or anyone else, but being better does not guarantee great success. There are so many intangibles that the consumer looks for and it is ever changing. For instance, great food used to be the critical element of a restaurant, but today, experience can outweigh the food. Don't become a commodity that consumers can easily replace. If you are known as an innovator and for doing the right things, you will end up with loyal customers who will spread the word to others.

Different is better than better. This thought will keep you motivated to continue to look at what other brands are doing that you can learn from. With this new knowledge, you can innovate and make your brand one that the industry looks at as a leader.

Key Takeaways: Different is Better than Better: How do you keep your brand current.

"The whole mentality of approaching your business with what's next is one of the secrets to long-term success. When you look at today's industry leaders, they are taking great brands, improving them and then developing new brands. Despite their successes, they are not waiting for a pat on the back."

1. **Differentiate yourself.**
   - Honesty and integrity are where you start.
   - Build a culture where your team has clear direction and the opportunity to make a difference.
   - Be a forward thinker and not someone who focuses on the past, whether positive or negative.

2. **Differentiate your brand.**
   - Listen to your customers and your team to evaluate what you need to work on to stay relevant.
   - Make the experience special. Whatever that means, your guests need to look at your brand as memorable.
   - Create key differentiators and be prepared to adjust. Others will copy what you do well.

3. **Overcome obstacles and recognize your breaks.**
   - Obstacles become opportunities and opportunities have solutions.
   - Things happen that you can't control at the time. Don't dwell on negative situations. Focus on positive solutions.
   - Network and make your own breaks, but realize that your successes will be watched and others will try to race by you.

4. **Watch and learn and then innovate.**
   - Listen, watch, read, and do whatever it takes to stay current.
   - No idea is a bad idea. Encourage others to generate creative thoughts. It does not take much to come up with the next great innovative idea.

- Stay open-minded. As hard as it is to admit that some proven winners are getting tired, realize that you did it before and you will do it again.

When you want to say you are better than someone else or you hear someone else say it, ask why? Within that answer, there should be something that clearly states that you are different.

ABOUT THE AUTHOR

Bruce Reinstein is a hospitality industry executive who grew up working in his family's restaurant business, starting when he was 13 years old. He then went on to attend the Cornell University School of Hotel Administration.

Bruce worked for Hyatt Hotels out of college where had the opportunity to learn from some great industry leaders. His work ethic and desire to continue to improve moved him quickly up the ladder. It also gave him the opportunity to understand the importance of giving back to others based on what he learned from his mentors.

One of his greatest pleasures was coming back home to Boston to join his father David, and brothers Eliot and Larry, in growing the Souper Salad brand. In 1996, Bruce and his brother Larry started Fresh City and built it into a national concept, which was awarded the Nation's Restaurant News Hot Concepts Award. Fresh City was truly an innovative brand that was a leader in the Fast-Casual revolution.

In 2011, after selling the Fresh City concept, Bruce was fortunate to become president of Consolidated Concepts, a company he grew to more than 200 clients. He currently is the founder of Big Splash Advisors where he focuses on bold and innovative foodservice solutions. He continues to look for the next chapter that will make a difference for both himself and the professional people he is able to work with.

Working hard with a determination to be successful and to make a difference has come as the result of the love and support of his wife Jayne, and children Michael and Amanda, which he will always be grateful for.